Praise for the first edition of *The Best Damn Web Marketing* Checklist, Period!

Stoney's Web Marketing Checklist should be by the side of every regardless of their level of experience. If this doesn't save you lots of time a make you tons of money I don't know what will. If you haven't bought the book yet, what are you waiting for?

Jeffrey Eisenberg
Author of New York Times Bestsellers *Call to Action* and *Waiting for Your Cat to Bark*

Checklists on steroids! Stoney's *Best Damn Web Marketing Checklist, Period!* is going to be attached to you from the first page and follow you around wherever you go until your online business dreams come true. I have always been a checklist and cheat sheet fanatic. There never seem to be enough of them, and they are always spread out in various places. Stoney compiled and organized 36 checklists, with more than 675 action points, along with examples, and he explains the reasoning behind each recommendation. Not only do you get the checklists with descriptive information, but you can download a quickie cheat sheet to apply to a number of websites. Everybody will want this book.

Kim Krause Berg
Usability and User Experience Analyst, Internet Marketing Ninjas;
Founder and Administrator, Cre8asiteforums

If you ever feel confused about today's complex marketing landscape, you're not alone. Even an experienced online publisher like me sometimes feels overwhelmed. *The Best Damn Web Marketing Checklist, Period!* cuts through the complexity and demystifies online marketing, breaking it down into achievable steps. Stoney is the real deal and communicates in everyday language. You'll learn exactly what steps you need to take to create a Class A online presence that attracts customers and contributes to your bottom line.

Anita Campbell
Founder, CEO and Publisher of *Small Business Trends*

OMG! Stoney's checklist just saved me from having to read at least 10 different web marketing books. Not only did he summarize the most important items to focus on, he tells you why. I don't have to take notes and I can just benchmark against his checklist. This is an invaluable time saver as well as informative on best practices that your website cannot live without if you want to compete online today.

Shirley Tan
Author of *Ecom Hell* and Ecommerce Consultant

I'm impressed! I'm a fan of checklists to make sure that nothing is forgotten in creating and setting up sites and marketing campaigns, and this book has you covered. From domain selection to site structure to marketing campaigns, these checklists will make sure you don't miss any crucial steps in your search for digital success. Thank you, Stoney, for creating these lists; they are indispensable.

Brad Geddes
Founder of Certified Knowledge and
Author of *Advanced Google AdWords*

There's a wealth of solid, actionable advice in Stoney's *Best Damn Web Marketing Checklist, Period!*, and it's expressed in clear, concise nuggets that are easy to understand and follow. It's a fast, easy way for online marketers of every discipline to make sure they're adhering to the best practices — and learn some insider tips and tricks along the way. Stoney's created a master reference work that belongs on every web marketer's shelf!

David Szetela
Owner and CEO of FMB Media

Stoney has covered everything necessary for creating a powerful web presence online. It's definitely a daunting task to create a web presence from scratch, but *The Best Damn Web Marketing Checklist, Period!* tells you everything you need to know, from infrastructure issues to mobile to social marketing and then some. An excellent resource.

Tamar Weinberg
Digital Marketing Strategist and Author of
The New Community Rules: Marketing on the Social Web

SEO, PPC, CSS, URLs and CTAs — the acronyms alone that are thrown around in web marketing can be confusing. How do you put it all together and make it work for your site? Enter Stoney's checklist, your new best friend. This is your handy reference guide to building your web presence the right way, all in one convenient guide.

Barry Schwartz
News Editor at Search Engine Land and CEO of RustyBrick

Stoney lays out everything you need to rank your website online and gives action plans for it all. If you're looking for strategy to building your business online, pay detailed attention to *The Best Damn Web Marketing Checklist, Period!*

John Rampton
Managing Editor at Search Engine Journal

For years now I have been reading Stoney's articles and blog posts online. Not only do I enjoy his writing style, I have always been able to learn something new from his experience and expertise. So when he decided to expand his original 2007 marketing checklist into a concise book format, I was thrilled. Within the pages of this book is a wealth of information covering just about every aspect of online and digital marketing, all penned from one of the industry's leading experts. With its easy-to-digest checklist style format, every online marketer worth their salt will want to not only own this book, but keep it handy when developing and implementing marketing campaigns. It is written in such a way that both the layman and advanced person will greatly benefit from the knowledge within.

David Wallace
Co-Founder and CEO of SearchRank

Understanding SEO is a mystery to many; however, it is of the utmost importance to all businesses. If you are on Page 2 of Google, you're essentially invisible. Stoney's book shows you step-by-step everything you need to do to ensure you dominate the search results and show up on Page 1.

Melonie Dodaro
Social Media Speaker and Author at Top Dog Social Media

As a link builder, the Links & Buttons Checklist is truly invaluable for anyone who seeks to create a great user experience through hyperlinks. I love the format of the entire piece, as it breaks each to-do item down and uses simple language that's perfect for the novice or expert marketer. The entire book should serve as a comprehensive resource for anyone marketing online today.

Julie Joyce
Owner and Director of Operations at Link Fish Media

This book will prove to be a must-have resource for marketers and web developers alike. It's the most comprehensive checklist I've seen to date. No site audit should be performed without it.

Annie Cushing
Blogger at Annielytics.com

Incredibly comprehensive, A to Z guideline for creating a new — or revamping an existing— web property. Stoney's checklists cover all the bases, from architecture and design to content optimization, providing easy-to-understand definitions and examples. A terrific primer for anyone new to the field, and a great reminder of best practices for more seasoned digital marketers.

Michelle Robbins
Vice President, Technology at Third Door Media, Inc.

I wish this book had been on my bookshelf many times over the last 10 years. What Stoney has done is take his vast experience in internet marketing and compiled a book of cheat sheets that provide the reader a roadmap to building a web presence, optimizing it, and strategically promoting it. This is a must have for any digital marketing strategist.

Patrick Schaber
Senior Director of Marketing at Intertech

I've always been a fan of checklists. It's rare to find an online marketing book both simple and comprehensive. By his use of checklists, Stoney makes a complex set of knowledge very approachable. This is a must for any serious online marketer's bookshelf. The individual checklists form a great foundation for aspiring marketers to learn and understand the technical and human factors of online marketing.

Will Scott
CEO of Search Influence

I've known Stoney for years now, and have always been a big fan of his checklists. This is one book that will have a permanent spot on my desk, as I'll always refer to it when performing SEO audits of websites.

Bill Hartzer
Senior SEO Strategist at Globe Runner

Ask anyone here at Vertical Measures, I've been pushing for checklists to help run our business from the first day we started. But it's not always easy; you're too busy to stop and create them, things change, etc. But now Stoney is laying them right in our laps. There is a checklist for everything web marketing in this book. And not just checklists, but nice explanations for each one. I know our company will use this, and I bet yours can too!

Arnie Kuenn
CEO of Vertical Measures and Author of *Accelerate!*

This checklist is really handy. I don't think I've ever seen anything as comprehensive as this. And then I thought: Why not!? Checklists are the way all complex projects are delivered effectively. Stoney has always been a trusted and respected leader in the digital marketing world, and his list is comprehensive and accurate. You can take his suggestions to the bank. If you have a website, you need this checklist.

Sage Lewis
Author of *Link Building Is Dead. Long Live Link Building!*

Finding a genuinely comprehensive online marketing list is extremely rare. Finding one that is also accurate, current and yet actionable for a non-geek website owner is truly a unique experience. Stoney writes with the kind of insight and topical breadth that comes only from experience gained doing the work over many years. This is a collection of earned wisdom, not the empty theory that often dominates the online marketing world. Every business owner should keep a copy of this checklist on hand for their own benefit, and to help in qualifying potential vendors.

Ryan Freeman
President of Strider Search Marketing

With *The Best Damn Web Marketing Checklist, Period!*, Stoney has delivered a thorough, well-researched, and insightful exploration of the latest web marketing principles and techniques in a practical and enjoyable book that pushes the boundaries of the art and science of successful website marketing. Filled with helpful checklists and actionable procedures, Stoney's book is an invaluable resource that ought to be required reading for anyone serious about web marketing.

Brett Tabke
Founder and CEO of Pubcon

The Best Damn Web Marketing Checklist, Period! is a comprehensive and actionable analysis of a successful website design, web development, usability and SEO, summarized in an easy-to-understand checklist. It's all you need to build a solid foundation for an impressive online presence for your business. Use this roadmap to build a brand new website or evaluate and improve an existing one. The book is packed with actionable tips — not just best practices, but advice aimed at success.

Lyena Solomon
Online Search Specialist

Stoney's Web Marketing Checklist has to be the most comprehensive list of internet marketing items I have seen anyone put together. I plan on fully integrating his checklist into my proposals and strategies. It lives up to its name of *The Best Damn Web Marketing Checklist, Period!*

Scott Polk
Founder of ObsidianEdge

There are three key reasons why Stoney deGeyter's book is *The Best Damn Web Marketing Checklist, Period!* First, his 35 checklists will help you to avoid the pitfalls. Second, his 675+ action points tell you how to seize the opportunities. Third, his book is only 200+ pages long, so you can make $1,000s in increased sales and still get back home by six o'clock.

Greg Jarboe
President of SEO-PR and Author of *YouTube and Video Marketing: An Hour a Day*

The Best Damn
Web Marketing Checklist,
Period!
2.0

by Stoney deGeyter

Velocitized Media
Uniontown, Ohio

Published by: Velocitized Media, Uniontown, OH 44685

Velocitized Media is the publishing division of Pole Position Marketing, 9841 Cleveland Ave. NW, Uniontown, Ohio 44685

Books may be purchased by contacting the publisher and author at: info@polepositionmarketing.com

Cover Design by: Chelsea Melaragno, www.asketchymind.com

Editors: Julie Graff, Deb Briggs and Kathy Gray

deGeyter, Stoney, 1972-

The Best Damn Web Marketing Checklist, Period! 2.0

Library of Congress Control Number: 2014940796

1. Business 2. Internet 3. Web Marketing

ISBN 978-0-9903461-4-2

Second Edition Printed in the United States of America

To you, and every internet marketer who knows they can't do it on their own.

TABLE OF CONTENTS

FOREWORD

There are a staggering number of details in this business. From content to code, design to distribution, there are literally thousands of little things that combine to create a marketing outcome. And each one of them has an impact. Some little things can make a huge difference. And sometimes, the things that seem big hardly move the needle at all.

And all of these little marketing details are cumulative. It's a game of inches. The more aspects we do well, the more demand we generate. Realizing this is both thrilling and depressing, these two thoughts are almost simultaneous: *"I can make a difference"* and *"I have one million things to do."*

That's why marketers are overwhelmed. We are frustrated and confused. *What to do next? Or where to even begin?*

Enter Stoney deGeyter. The book you are holding is empowering in two ways. It's an exhaustive list of many hundreds of those important details. A list so thorough, it could only have been created by a professional with 20+ years of experience. This is the combination of tens of thousands of hours of hands-on marketing experience. There is just no way that anyone but an absolute pro could have captured all of this in one place.

But the format is just as important as the content. This is the most accessible marketing book you'll ever read. There is zero fluff. There's no theory. There are no extra words. It's just dozens of checklists. This foreword is the wordiest and least practical part of this book. Every page after this one is pure practicality. Probably, you should stop reading this now and just turn the page.

Still here? Then I'll wrap this up. In hospitals, checklists save lives. This book won't do that, but it will save years of toil, frustration, and weak results. So go to the page for the marketing aspect you're focused on today and put it into practice. Then get a copy for any colleague, friend, or family member involved in a marketing role. They'll thank you for it. There's gold on every page.

Andy Crestodina
Author of *Content Chemistry: The Illustrated Handbook for Content Marketing*

ABOUT THE AUTHOR

Stoney deGeyter started doing "web stuff" in 1998. Initially diving into website design and development, it was his dad, Andy, who pushed him in the direction of web marketing. Or as Stoney likes to call it, Web Presence Optimization.

Pole Position Marketing was started in Stoney's bedroom and quickly expanded to his living room. Fast forward several years and Pole Position Marketing (PPM) is one of the longest-lasting web marketing companies today. Stoney attributes that to his focus on web marketing strategies that are good for growing a business, not just its search engine rankings.

He is also a firm believer that web marketing is just too big for one person to know it all at an expert level. Stoney has always focused on building a team of experts, each within their own area of web marketing: Social, content, analytics, SEO, PPC, conversions, etc.

While there is a great deal of overlap between each of these areas, having experts in each discipline allows PPM to create an effective—and complete—approach to all of their clients' web marketing campaigns. Jack of all trades, master of none? Not in this house!

Stoney has been on the speaking circuit for years, appearing at national industry conferences such as Pubcon, Search Engine Strategies (SES), Search Marketing Expo (SMX), Affiliate Summit, Public Relations Society of America (PRSA), and International Association of Business Communicators (IABC).

Stoney's articles about how to navigate the web marketing landscape have been published on *Search Engine Land*, *Search Engine Journal* and *Visibility Magazine*, and he is occasionally quoted in WSJ.com. He also shares how to "velocitize" your web marketing efforts on the company blog: www.PolePositionMarketing.com/emp.

Contact Stoney for web marketing strategy, to speak at your conference, seminar or workshop, and/or provide in-house training for your team at www.PolePositionMarketing.com, or by phone at 866-685-3374.

ACKNOWLEDGEMENTS

As in the first edition of this book, I want to give thanks, first and foremost, to God, for giving me breath, without which I would not have life. To Jesus, for giving me salvation, without which I would have only this life to look forward to. To the Holy Spirit, for giving me guidance, without which I would not be able to enjoy this life with a true moral compass. And for God's grace and mercy that allows me to have a relationship with Him despite how flawed I truly am.

Second, I would like to thank my wife, Maria, for her love and encouragement. I could have no better business, family and life partner than her. I love you.

I want to extend many thanks to the Pole Position Marketing Pit Crew. Their contributions to this book were invaluable and it would not be complete without them. It's their knowledge and expertise I relied on where mine lacked. They were also the first people I went to when it came time to updating this book. Thank you!

Finally, I would like to thank my friends in the web marketing industry who have supported me through the years, and everyone I have never met who have published their thoughts, ideas and findings for all to read. So much of my knowledge over the years is a direct result of your labor.

INTRODUCTION

SEO IS MARKETING

Many online marketers are coming to the realization that search is far less relevant today than it was even just a few years ago. That's not because fewer people are searching. On the contrary, more people are searching more often to find the information they are looking for. What's changed, however, is the nature of search itself.

Search is no longer just done on a search engine. And engaging with your visitors isn't just a matter of picking up the phone or answering an email. Search and engagement is everywhere, and as search engines continue to adapt, they are using these off-site signals to determine the relevance of a site to the visitor's needs.

Ranking #1 is all but extinct anymore as every searcher gets a different set of results. If you're number one for your keywords, congratulations! Now turn off your personalized results and see if you are still there. Yes? Congratulations again. Now go use someone else's profile in another part of the country and perform the search again. Chances are, you're no longer in the top spot.

And why should you be? What is relevant to you isn't necessarily relevant to Joe Schmoe somewhere else, who has entirely different interests and a different group of people recommending different products that might meet his needs.

But it's not just about search either. Jane Schmoe is getting recommendations she didn't even know she needed as she scrolls through her Twitter and Facebook streams. She's also connecting with "experts" in your area of expertise via LinkedIn. On top of that, she's finding products that pique her interest on Instagram and Pinterest. All of these are more relevant to her than your site that shows up #1 in Google. Why? Because they are essentially recommendations made by people she trusts. At least, people she trusts more than someone she's never engaged with before.

SEO isn't dead, and it never will die. But it's less important to online success. It's less important, even, for top search engine rankings, whatever that might mean today or tomorrow. Web marketing, digital marketing or web presence optimization—whatever you want to call it—requires a more holistic approach. It's not one thing; it's everything. You can pick and choose where you will invest and engage, but you can no longer invest in SEO alone and expect to succeed.

THIS BOOK HAS A HISTORY

I started writing the 2014 edition of this book way back in 2007. Initially published as a series of blog posts and then later compiled into a PDF ebook, it was by far the most popular piece of content I've ever written. I wish I had kept accurate stats on this, but I don't think I'm overstating to say it's been viewed, read, and downloaded tens of thousands of times over the years.

I've known for some time that the original checklists were due for an update, but I never carved out the time to make it happen. Well, now I have. Twice.

If there is one constant over the years, it's that the web changes. Fast. What was web marketing back when I started bears little resemblance to what is web marketing today. Much in the same way that a picture of a prospering city 100 years ago no longer represents that same city today, the web marketing landscape has grown in more ways than we could have ever dreamed.

Many of the foundational, bedrock principles of online marketing still remain today, but what has been built on that foundation continues to evolve, grow, expand, disappear and morph as new technologies emerge, new ways of getting information are invented and an increasing number of digital communities are born. At its core, however, is the web and the websites that are built on it.

This book you are holding is more than just another SEO checklist, or a simple "revision" of the blog posts published in 2007 that carry the same name. In fact, if I may be so bold, I believe this truly is the best damn web marketing checklist you'll ever read. Period!

The 2014 edition saw the addition of 13 new checklists and over 200 new action points, tackling areas such as social media, analytics, PPC, mobile design, etc. Moreover, unlike the original ebook, the full-length version included expanded introductions and explanations, providing a much more detailed understanding of why each matters.

We intentionally focused on the "what to dos" rather than the "how tos" in the 2014 edition as the former changes less quickly than the latter. And overall, the 2014 version has held up pretty well. As I went through it, I found the overall concepts had stood the test of those three long years.

Still, there have been changes and new developments, and this edition addresses those. In addition to updating each and every checklist, I expanded the checklists on ecommerce concerns, mobile optimization, and local optimization and added a checklist on video optimization. Rest assured, if you had the 2014 version, you will find plenty new to discover here. And if this is your first experience with *The Best Damn Web Marketing Checklist, Period!*, well let's just say this book is going to keep you very, very busy for awhile.

FOR BEST RESULTS...

Overall, you're holding not just a series of checklists, but a book of procedures, ideas and best practices all designed to help you improve your website and just about every area of your online marketing efforts.

There is no need to read this book straight through. While I have organized the checklists in somewhat of a chronological fashion (i.e., design comes before code), each checklist is fully self-contained. You will find some points that make an appearance in one or more checklists and other content that may feel eerily similar as you read it. This is intentional.

You are encouraged to jump around from list to list, as needed, to complete whatever phase of marketing you are currently working through on your website. It's a good idea to be familiar with all checklist topics offered in this book so you'll have the opportunity to seek out more detailed information when necessary, but I would advise you not to ignore any section of this book simply because you're beyond that particular phase in marketing your site. There is no doubt that you'll find something in each list that you hadn't thought to do during your initial site development or redevelopment processes.

As detailed as these checklists are, however, they will never be fully complete. I tried to avoid specific information that I know will become outdated soon. I can't tell you how to set up Google Analytics, Facebook or an autoresponder account because those things change almost daily. In fact, I pretty much avoid telling you how to do anything, focusing instead on what needs to be done.

This isn't a technical guide meant only for the computer geeks who pump out code all day. This is a series of checklists for the marketing manager, site owner, social media strategist, SEO, link builder, content writer and administrative assistant. This book is for anyone who is in charge of any area of a website and needs to know what they can do to improve their web presence. You may or may not be the person responsible for making it all happen, or you might be the person who directs the people who do. This book arms you with the information you need to ensure what needs to get done, does, in fact, get done.

This is the layman's checklist. It's your checklist. Some of the points here might be a bit technical or even go somewhat above your head, but that's OK. The checklists contained herein give you the information you need to tell the people who do the implementation exactly what you want to see, and helps you explain to them why it's necessary. Once these checklists are employed, the only argument against implementation that remains will be "that's not possible." To which you should quickly agree and then escort that person out the door so you can find their replacement. Preferably someone who knows that in today's programming environment, everything is possible.

If you're looking for some secret formula to online success, you won't find it in these pages. Sorry. I won't tell you how to beat Google's algorithm, or how to shoot to the top of the search engine rankings. But what I do give you is plenty of website marketing actionables that will keep your marketing and development teams busy for quite some time.

Web marketing is a series of baby steps. Some get you further than others, but it's mostly a lot of little things that add up to something big. Very big. The points here are your baby steps. Take them slow, or fast, it doesn't matter. Go at a pace that works for your company, but by all means, just keep taking one baby step after the next!

BUT WAIT, THERE'S MORE!

While this book gives you plenty of explanation to go along with each point, sometimes you just want a list of actionables to pass around. So I have created *The Best Damn Web Marketing Cheat Sheet!*, which contains all the check points from this book with the commentary stripped out. It's set into a nice printable format for easy viewing and reference. Of course, you can always refer back to this book for more explanation whenever you need to make your case!

You can download the cheat sheet at: WebMarketingChecklist.com

The Pole Position Marketing Pit Crew is always standing by to help as well. Expert advice is just a phone call away: 866-685-3374.

DOMAIN NAME & URLS

> …people spend 24% of their gaze time looking at the URLs in the search results.[1]
>
> –Jakob Nielsen
> Nielsen Norman Group

What This Checklist Is About

This checklist covers various aspects of your website's primary and secondary domain names and the URL structure you use for internal pages of the site. I'll show you how domain names should be used and what you need to ensure proper site and browser functionality, giving you the best marketing advantage through your site URLs.

Why Domains and URLs Are Important

"What will our domain name be?" is one of the first things people ask themselves when starting a new online business. Or at least it should be! In fact, your domain name should be considered *before* you even choose your business name. If the business name you choose doesn't have an available domain name, you may be crippling your online marketing efforts before they even begin.

The domain name you ultimately choose—and the resulting consequences—can have a vast impact on your long-term marketing efforts. Long or hard-to-remember domain names can be the death toll for any website. Short or clever business names (such as Grafix4u) may be easy to remember, but getting people to remember how the URL is spelled is another story altogether.

Your domain name is the key to the identity of your online business. The domain name you choose will have a significant impact on your brand identity, and, to a lesser extent, your keyword ranking performance. If you do not yet have an established business, you may want to wait on choosing a business name until after you have found an available domain name.

Aside from your domain name, you also have to pay attention to the URLs you use for your internal site pages. Letting your web developers program your URLs with no thought to their usability, marketability, or search engine friendliness can suppress your online exposure, preventing your target customers from more easily finding your website.

DOMAIN & URLS CHECKLIST

❏ SHORT AND MEMORABLE URL

Shorter domains can be easier to remember than longer domains, provided they make sense to the reader. The longer your domain name, the more apt someone is to get it wrong when they type it into the URL or search bar. When that happens, the best case scenario is they don't find your site. Worst case is they find your competitor's site instead.

One-word domain names are best, provided it's a word that can be easily spelled. However, there are times when the perfect one-word domain name isn't available. When that is the case, keeping your domain name to fewer than three words is ideal.

> **Examples**
> No: *creative-widget-solution-factory.com*
> Yes: *widgetfactory.com*
> Yes: *widgets.com*

❏ PURCHASE A .COM TLD

Unless you operate exclusively in a country that has its own top-level domain (TLD), the .com TLD is going to serve you best. Even if you want to use an alternate TLD for stylistic or branding purposes, you're still better off owning the .com as well. Many people instinctively type in ".com" instead of other domain extensions, even when they are told otherwise. Without the .com, it's very possible you'll lose traffic to another website.

❏ BUY MULTIPLE TLD EXTENSIONS

While the .com TLD is the most common, there are many other TLDs available; some more valuable than others. Securing alternate TLD versions of your domain can help you secure your brand name, keeping a competitor from throwing up a website to piggy back off your hard-built brand marketing.

Unless you're fanatical about brand protection, you won't necessarily need (or want) every TLD available. In most cases, buying up a couple of the most popular TLDs is enough to secure your business from domain brand poachers of any consequence.

Here is a list of top level domain name options worth considering:

- ❏ .COM
- ❏ .NET
- ❏ .INFO
- ❏ .ORG
- ❏ .BIZ
- ❏ .CO
- ❏ INDUSTRY-SPECIFIC TLDs
- ❏ COUNTRY SPECIFIC TLDs

❏ SECURE MULTIPLE DOMAIN SPELLINGS

When purchasing your domain name(s), you also want to look at purchasing alternative versions that will help secure your brand name. This includes any domains that poachers might pick up, or something someone might accidentally type in when trying to reach your site.

- ❏ HYPHENATIONS (pole-position-marketing.com)
- ❏ MISSPELLINGS (polepostionmarketing.com)
- ❏ MISUNDERSTANDINGS (pullpositionmarketing.com)

❏ KEYWORDS IN URLs

When you use keywords in your domain name, you help the search engines "understand" what your site is about before they even crawl the first page. It also helps produce natural keyword links when other websites link to you using your URL, which may slightly enhance your ability to rank in the search results.

Using your keywords in your business name is the easiest way to work search keywords into your URL. If you already have keywords in your business name, or are in the process of choosing a business name, now is the time to think about this option. Otherwise, you may just have to see if you can work a keyword into your URL before buying it. This is something you want to do subtly and only as it makes sense for your company.

Example
No: *UniquePower.com*
Yes: *BatteryStuff.com*

❏ Secure Type-In Keyword URLs

Most browsers have only one bar for typing in both search keywords and URLs. You can capitalize on this by purchasing domain names that contain product names, brand names or any other words that your target audience might be searching for.

Often a search is nothing more than a keyword with a .com added to it! Purchase any URLs that you feel may be frequently, randomly, or even accidentally typed in.

Example
dogbeds.com
dogdoors.com
dogtoys.com

❏ Redirect Alternate Domains

Any and all alternative domain names you purchase need to redirect back to your primary domain. Without this redirect in place, the value of holding an alternate domain is limited to brand protection only. However, implementing a proper 301 redirect for each domain name will send visitors to your site every time one is typed into the location or search bar.

Important note: Be sure to use 301 redirects on all alternate domains. Any other redirect (or "parking" the domain) creates a non-search-friendly redirect that can hurt your online marketing efforts later.

Example
batteryjunk.com redirects to *batterystuff.com*
batreystuff.com redirects to *batterystuff.com*

❏ Use Domain Email Addresses

When setting up an email address to use for your business, always use a business-branded email address. This provides a cohesive communication format that lends credibility to your business while also reinforcing your brand name.

There are plenty of free email services such as Gmail, Yahoo, Hotmail, etc., that are great for managing your personal email. These should only be used for business provided you can send and receive your business branded email through them as well.

Example
No: *pimpmcfly@gmail.com*
No: *mybusiness@gmail.com*
Yes: *stoney@polepositionmarketing.com*

❏ REDIRECT NON-WWW URLs

Search engines have a tendency to look at every distinct URL as a unique page, even if the content on the pages is exactly the same. Eventually, they "figure out" that the URLs should be treated as one, but until they do, you can wind up splitting the value of your pages between each URL version, even if the content is exactly the same.

One of the biggest culprits of this problem (there are several that will be addressed in later chapters) is the www vs. non-www version of a URL. Decide which option you want to use throughout your site and set up 301 redirects from the version you don't want to the version that you do. This will ensure the search engines index and value only the proper version, while visitors are also being redirected so they can bookmark or socialize the correct URL as well.

Tip: Be sure all internal site links point to only the correct URL.

Example
site.com redirects to *www.site.com* (or vice versa)

❏ ASSIGN CANONICAL URLs

Many sites are built using content management systems that allow a single page of content to be accessed multiple ways, each creating a unique URL for the visitor. This creates duplicate content that is problematic to search engine indexing and ranking. The best solution is to code your site so there is only one possible URL for any given piece of content or product information. It might require a bit of extra programming, but it's a fix worth the expense.

As a band-aid solution, search engines allow you to set a "canonical" URL for any duplicate content. This canonical tag can be placed in the code of all duplicate pages to inform the engines which is the proper URL to attribute all ranking or link value to.

Example
URL:*http://www.site.com/product/duplicate-canonical-page.html*
Tag: `<link rel="canonical" href="http://www.site.com/`
`     product/canonical-page.html"/>`

❏ REDIRECT HOME PAGE TO ROOT

Your home page should be accessible via the root domain only, not the actual page file name. Regardless of the actual file name or the location of your home page, create a 301 redirect back to the root level. Also be sure that all internal site links use only the root URL as well, not the page file name.

Example
www.site.com/index.html redirects to *www.site.com*
All links point to: *www.site.com*

❏ ORGANIZE URLS

Don't place all your pages into the root directory. Instead, create appropriate category and sub-category groupings that will keep your content organized in a consistent URL structure. This structure helps visitors and search engines identify the page's topical relevance within the site by looking at the URL alone.

Examples
No: *www.site.com/pet-doors.html*
       www.site.com/dog-doors.html
       www.site.com/large-dog-doors.html
       www.site.com/small-dog-door.html
       www.site.com/cat-doors.html
Yes: *www.site.com/pet-doors/*
       www.site.com/pet-doors/dog-doors/
       www.site.com/pet-doors/dog-doors/large-dog-doors.html
       www.site.com/pet-doors/dog-doors/small-dog-doors.html
       www.site.com/pet-doors/cat-doors.html

❏ KEYWORDS IN DIRECTORY NAMES

When implementing your file structure for categories, sub-categories, and pages on your website, use keywords wherever applicable. Remove useless words such as "store," "category," "product," etc., and replace those with category and product names. Using keywords in directory names provides a nice visual indicator of what page the visitor is viewing, while also giving the search engines a hint of the content of the page.

Example
No: */category2568/subcat12/product8954.html*
Yes: */battery-chargers/samlex-chargers/samlex-24v-battery-charger.html*

❏ HYPHENS BETWEEN WORDS

When choosing a file structure for all your pages, images, and web documents, it is best practice to separate words with hyphens rather than underscores or spaces. Hyphens are more visually appealing than underscores, which when underlined can look like spaces in the URLs.

Search engines tend to interpret hyphens as a space between words while underscores are treated as no separation at all. Using hyphens helps the search engines "read" the URL properly. Also, hyphens ensure the full URL is readable to the visitor.

> **Examples**
> No: */battery_chargers.html*
> No: */battery tutorial download.pdf*
> Yes: */battery-chargers.html*
> Yes: */battery-tutorial-download.pdf*

❏ STATIC OVER DYNAMIC URLs

Dynamic URLs are less of a problem today than they were ten years ago. However, search engines may opt not to index URLs with more than two or three query strings. When using dynamic URLs, keep the query strings to a maximum of three, or better yet, convert them to static URLs.

❏ HTTPS OVER HTTP

Secure URLs aren't just for shopping carts anymore! Search engines have made site security a ranking factor, which means that all your site URLs should be running securely via HTTPS rather than HTTP. Unfortunately, just switching to HTTPS can be complicated, so be sure to work with your developer and web marketing provider to ensure a smooth transition.

❏ REGISTER DOMAIN FOR 5+ YEARS

If you expect your business to survive for the long-haul, go ahead and register your domain for an extended period of time. While there are far, far more important ranking signals to focus on, it certainly can't hurt to demonstrate confidence in your own longevity. Short URL registration periods can be an indication that you lack long-term viability. Against other indicators, search engines may use short registration against you. A domain registered for many years is more likely to provide a confident outlook on the site's long-term prospects. At the very worst, it won't matter at all.

DESIGN CONSIDERATIONS

Today, anything that's fixed and unresponsive isn't web design, it's something else. If you don't embrace the inherent fluidity of the web, you're not a web designer, you're something else.[2]

–Andrew Clarke
Stuff & Nonsense

WHAT THIS CHECKLIST IS ABOUT

This checklist covers various visual aspects of your website that are usually factored in during the design and development process. Much of the information in this list is pulled from industry "best practices" that have been batted around the web for years. Not all the items mentioned here will be relevant for your site in particular, and some may even be wrong for a website in your industry. However, the points listed here represent a good starting point when looking to improve the design aspects of your site.

WHY DESIGN IS IMPORTANT

Your website is one of the first impressions that someone will get of your business. This means that the design of your site—how it looks and feels, how visitors interact with it, etc.—is critical to making a good first impression, not to mention keeping the visitor engaged from start to finish.

There is more to good website design than great eye appeal. Unfortunately, eye appeal is too often the primary, if not the only, goal of website designers. A website is far more than an informational brochure; it is an interactive experience with your company, services, products and more.

The more you design your website to fulfill this interactive role, the more likely you are to have a website that actually generates money for your business. In fact, a properly built and designed website is an effective marketing tool that returns far more than it "costs" to create.

Great websites are built upon a base of industry-standard "best practices" that web users have come to expect. Venture too far outside of these practices and you run the risk of confusing, if not outright annoying, your visitors. As web user expectations morph and change over time, best practices can change as well. All best practices should be implemented with a grain of salt and a high dose of testing to ensure each has a net positive effect on your website.

Overall, you have to do what is right for your website and your visitors. Nothing should be sacred if a better way is found (and proven). If you have an existing site, look for ways to implement and test these considerations. If you are designing a new site, look to implement these points from the onset, and then test variations moving forward as a means to continue to improve upon past successes.

DESIGN CONSIDERATIONS CHECKLIST

❏ MESSAGING BEFORE DESIGN

Most websites are designed without factoring in the content that will be populating the site. In these instances, a template is created and the content is built to fit the space that was designed for it. This is a backward approach. The design should fit the needs of the content, not the other way around.

When you start with your content, you can ensure that the site is designed with the messaging in mind. While you won't necessarily need a unique design for every page, you won't know what pages will require unique designs until you have the content. Once the site is designed, it's too late to go back else you run the risk of going over budget.

❏ TARGET YOUR AUDIENCE

Who is your audience and how do you reach them? Unfortunately, many sites are designed before this question is ever asked, when it should be asked— and answered— long before site development even starts.

By seeking the answer to this question first, you can learn how best to design your site for the audience that is most important for your business's success. This information will help you design the layout, choose primary colors, develop your navigation and write audience-targeted content and calls to action. Each of these will help you reach, attract and convert visitors that turn into customers.

❏ UNIQUE DESIGN

Your website design should be unique to you. Design templates can give you a great starting point; however, the finished website design should not look like any other site—even those that are using the same basic template as you. This is your chance to stand out. You can't do that when you look like the other guys.

❏ INSTANT SITE IDENTIFICATION

Do your visitors know what site they just landed on? Do they know what it is you offer? Can they tell that you provide the very solutions they're looking for? These are all questions that must be answered with a resounding "yes!"

Within a few seconds, each visitor must be able to immediately identify your company name, what you do, and determine that you offer exactly what they are looking for. If they can't, they will move on to a competitor's website instead. However, if that information is properly conveyed, then they'll spend their time on your site to find the information they came for.

❏ CLEAN AND CLUTTER-FREE DESIGN

Don't try to cram too much information onto a page. Many people make the mistake of thinking that visitors need to see as much information as possible—and have just as many options—in order to know what to do. The opposite is true.

Keep your choices and information as minimalistic as possible. Having too much information and too many options causes confusion that inhibits decision making. Creating fewer options helps visitors make better choices that will get them to the information they want faster.

❏ CONSISTENT PAGE LAYOUT

Keep a consistent design, using the same visual layout on all pages throughout the site. Page format changes are often jarring to the visitor, creating a less-than-pleasurable on-site experience. While there are times when page variations become necessary, they should not be so radically different that the visitor has to re-orientate himself to the changes. Keep every page as visually consistent as the next.

❏ CONSISTENT STYLING

Using cascading style sheets (CSS) makes it easy to keep your font, heading, images, colors and other styled elements consistent throughout the site. Changing styles from page to page creates a jarring disconnect for the visitor, rather than a seamless on-site browsing experience. You want to make sure that you maintain stylistic consistency that doesn't cause the visitor to be disengaged from the message.

❏ MINIMAL ON-PAGE STYLING

Almost all site styling can be handled via off-page CSS rather than on-page style code. Off-page CSS allows each page to load faster while creating a uniform style throughout the site. When on-page styles are needed for that rare occasion, keep them to a minimum and for elements that apply to that page only.

❏ MAINTAIN WHITE SPACE

Adding a little white space into your page design allows you to reduce clutter and highlight key features of the page at the same time. White space makes your pages easier to scan, read and understand, while also helping the visitor to focus on the action they should take next. Keep in mind, less white space equals more clutter. More white space equals less clutter.

❏ ELIMINATE DISTRACTIONS

All unnecessary distractions should be eliminated from the page design. This includes, but is not limited to, animations, goofy images, unnecessary links and even content that does not help fulfill the goals of the page. Anything that stands in the way of the visitors by distracting them from the conversion process must be eliminated.

❏ UNOBTRUSIVE BACKGROUND

The background of your website should be as unobtrusive as possible to keep the visitor focused on the page's content. There are some rare exceptions to this rule (a site that generates revenue from background ads, to name one), but for most sites, the content area is the primary space you want to draw attention to. The background's primary role is to help the visitor focus on the content area.

❏ MEET INDUSTRY BEST PRACTICES

Every industry tends to have its own set of best practices. This checklist is full of web-wide best practices, but best practices for your industry may vary. You must be sure you're designing your site to meet the expectations of the visitors who visit multiple sites in your industry. This could be as simple as adding specific types of content or could require some significant visual changes. Whatever it is, you want to be meeting and exceeding whatever expectations your visitors already have.

❏ EASY TO NAVIGATE

Navigational usability is a key aspect to ensuring your visitors can find what they want on your site quickly and easily. Many sites subscribe to the theory that if they put their entire sitemap in their main navigation then they have every option covered. Not so! Too many navigational options can confuse visitors and often keep them from fulfilling their objectives.

❏ DESCRIPTIVE HYPERLINKS

All links, whether part of the main navigation or scattered throughout your content, should accurately describe the destination page that you are linking to. You want to use search keywords in the link text that reflects each page's content. This helps both visitors and search engines know what the page is about (at least in part), just by reading the text of the link.

❏ VISUAL PAGE ORGANIZATION

How your content and page elements are organized can be crucial to ensuring your visitors can find the content they want quickly and easily. One way to organize your page layout is to create basic wireframe templates of all important pages as part of the design and development process. Wireframes let you move, add, and delete elements, helping you get the page layout just right. This ensures you get everything you need on each page and every on-page element has a proper place before any designing actually starts.

❏ CUSTOM 404 PAGE

When a visitor reaches your site via a bad link, or clicks a link that takes them to a broken URL, they are generally delivered to a white "page not found" screen. Create a custom 404 page that keeps visitors on a page that looks like the rest of your site.

This page should allow them to navigate just like any other page so they can continue on to find the information they were initially searching for. Be sure to provide some kind of "page not found" message, rather than delivering them to what looks like a legitimate—albeit irrelevant—page (such as the home page).

❏ FINDABLE PHONE NUMBER

Not everyone will find everything they need while browsing your website. Sometimes they simply don't know where to go, sometimes the information they need is not there, and sometimes they have questions that only a live person can answer to their satisfaction. Displaying your phone number on each page of your site can give visitors confidence that a live person is available if needed. That can make all the difference between gaining a customer and getting passed over for a more accessible competitor.

❏ LINK TO CONTACT INFORMATION

Even with a phone number clearly displayed, not every visitor will want to use the phone as their method of contacting you. Provide a clear link to a page with alternate contact information that gives the visitor multiple methods of reaching you. Don't hide this link in the footer, but keep it visible in your primary navigation so every visitor can easily find it.

❏ SCREEN-FRIENDLY FONT

There are a lot of fonts to choose from when developing your site, but not every font is great for reading on a screen. Most of the "traditional" fonts were designed for print, but now there are many fonts developed specifically for computer and tablet screens. To ensure your content is easier to read, choose screen-friendly fonts for your primary reading content.

❏ ADEQUATE FONT SIZE

Though many do not like large fonts due to the amount of space they consume, larger font sizes make your content easier to read. Smaller fonts can make the page look a lot tighter but are much more difficult on the eyes. If your content is valuable (and it should be) use a font size that is easily read by all visitors (both young and old). Don't make them work for it.

❏ RESIZABLE TEXT

Code your site so visitors are able to resize the text in their browser, based on their needs. Visitors with poor eyesight often enlarge text, making it easier for them to read. When this option isn't available, you force increased eye strain. You went through all that effort to write content; make sure your visitors don't have to struggle just to read it.

❏ NARROW PARAGRAPH TEXT

Wide paragraphs are extremely hard to read. When a reader's eyes finish one line, wide paragraphs make it difficult to find the next one without losing their place. Design your site so, regardless of screen size and resolution, the paragraphs don't become so wide that it affects the readability of the page. Content doesn't have to be newspaper-column narrow, but anything more than 6 to 8 inches wide increases reading difficulty.

❏ STRONG COLOR CONTRAST

Use colors that work well together but also are distinct enough to create visual contrast between various on-page elements. For example, yellow on white is typically difficult to see, but yellow works very well with black. Black on white offers the most contrast and should almost always be used for your primary text. Using contrasting colors on other areas of the page gives you the ability draw those areas out visually while still ensuring it's easy on the eyes to view.

❏ VISUAL COLORIZATION OF IMPORTANT ELEMENTS

A website doesn't have to be super-colorful to be effective. Quite the opposite. Sometimes even small amounts of color can really make a site pop. There are always some on-page elements that need to stand out over others. This is true for key areas you wish to highlight, links and calls to action, just to name three. Use colors wisely so that these important elements don't get lost in a sea of over-colorization or blend in with the blandness.

❏ NO SATURATED COLORS

Using colors that are extremely bright draw too much of the visitor's focus and are often difficult to look at. Bright colors can be used effectively; however, saturated colors should be avoided so each element of the page can receive its proper attention.

❏ USE ANIMATIONS WISELY

Website animations are an effective way to highlight key points or call attention to a specific area of your site. However, overuse of animations can come across as cheesy or unprofessional. Modern web technologies offer a lot of possibilities, but that doesn't mean they all need to be used. Keep page animation usage to a minimum, only to enhance the visitor experience. If they become annoying, you've gone way too far!

❏ INCORPORATE CALLS TO ACTION

Both your content and your visual design should include calls to action, action buttons, and other objects that give the visitor a clear indication of the next action they should take. These can be worked into navigation, headers, footers and textual areas. Use them wisely and be sure that you don't have competing actions that may confuse the visitor.

❏ DON'T REQUIRE BROWSER PLUGINS

For general site usage, avoid requiring visitors to download browser plugins in order to use the site properly. Such plugins can be useful for extra elements and goodies, but these should be unnecessary for general reading and interaction. Also keep mobile in mind. Many mobile browsers lack some of the basic functionality that computer browsers offer naturally.

❏ HIGH-DEFINITION IMAGES

We have moved far beyond the days of images displaying only at 72 dpi. In fact, many monitors and tablets now display at or near the high-def quality of televisions. Websites that employ low-quality images present a low-quality impression of their products or services. Using high-definition images ensures that your visitors can see your products cleanly and clearly, and your website as a whole looks and feels like you've joined the 21st century.

❏ OPTIMIZE IMAGES AND IMAGE USAGE

Graphics can be a great way to provide visual appeal and to highlight specific pieces of content. However, pages that overuse images can take longer to download than less image-heavy pages. While internet speeds are increasing, site download speeds are becoming increasingly important for search engine rankings and visitor experience. Do what you can to optimize your images to ensure the fastest page download speeds possible.

❏ READABLE IMAGE FILE NAMES

Using readable and keyword-friendly image file names helps both pages and images be found via relevant searches. Both can be a great source of relevant traffic and potential customers.

> **Example**
> No: */images/BDJ2330.jpg*
> Yes: */images/boys-denali-jacket.jpg*

❏ AVOID TEXT IN IMAGES

Placing text in images can add some visual flare that you may not be able to create otherwise. However, search engines, and visitors with images turned off, will be unable to read this important text. Be careful about the type of text you place in images to ensure your most important content is readable to search engines and people.

❏ PADDING AROUND IMAGES

Padding between images and text helps the image placement feel more natural. When text is too tight against an image, it can look as if the image was plopped onto the page as an afterthought. Proper padding gives your images room to breathe and makes the page look less cluttered.

❏ ADD TRUST SYMBOLS

Trust symbols can add a needed security element that helps visitors feel more confident about doing business with you. Images such as those provided by the Better Business Bureau, shopping cart security services and industry or local memberships, let visitors know that other trustworthy organizations have given your business an endorsement of some kind.

When possible, these trust symbols should be linked to a verification page that provides more information about the relationship between your two organizations. However, the presence of these symbols alone can go a long way toward helping your visitors feel confident that you are a company they can trust.

❏ "Skip" Multimedia and Ads

If you have multimedia or ad content that you want your visitors to experience, but it isn't critical to the conversion process, allow your visitors to easily skip it so they can more quickly access the content they want. Anytime a visitor is forced to wait more than a couple seconds to get to the information they desire, you are in danger of causing them to abandon your site. Make these distractions optional.

❏ No Browser Hi-Jacking

Let the visitor enjoy their own browsing experience rather than forcing them into an experience of your choosing. Causing new window pop-ups, automatic browser resizing, opening of new ad tabs, or replacing the page they go "back" to are all things that can easily aggravate a visitor. Forcing them into your preference over their own prevents the visitor from experiencing your site in a way they are most comfortable with and often leads to site abandonment.

❏ No Horizontal Scrolling

Be sure your visitors don't have to scroll horizontally to see yours page's content or information. This means you should use a variable rather than a fixed-width design. The only scrolling you want your visitors to do is vertical. There are some exceptions in modern design where elements of a page require a horizontal scroll to see more info. Netflix puts this to use effectively. However, for most sites, visitors won't think to or bother to scroll, so it's almost always best to avoid it when possible.

❏ Cross Browser Compatible

Every browser renders HTML and CSS differently. And as each browser comes out with updates, sites may display differently still. Your website needs to look and function properly in every major browser, including older versions of each. While not every browser or version will behave exactly the same, be sure that how your site looks and performs is acceptable, and your visitors won't notice any significant difference.

❏ Multi-Resolution Compatible

Different screens use different widths and resolutions. Your site should look good on all of them. If the visitor increases the font size, or magnifies their desktop viewing, that should not negatively impact the experience on your site. Don't rely on the visitor's computer to be set at specific resolutions for your site to function properly.

❏ MOBILE COMPATIBLE

There are not many instances where creating a separate mobile site makes sense. Instead, build a responsive website that is friendly to all kinds of mobile devices and screen widths. Responsive design ensures that all aspects of your site, from navigation to image sizes, react properly for each platform it is being viewed with, creating a better visitor experience on each device. AMP is a newer technology designed by Google specifically for mobile devices. Talk to your marketing team and developer as to whether AMP is the right approach for your website.

❏ PRINTER-FRIENDLY PAGES

When any page of your site is printed, be sure the result is clean and readable. Many sites are not printer friendly and produce wild results when a page is printed to paper. It's beneficial to use CSS to create printer-friendly outputs that can size text appropriately and eliminate unnecessary items such as navigation menus, which are useless in the printed format.

❏ INCORPORATE BREADCRUMBS

Incorporate breadcrumbs on all internal pages of your site. Breadcrumbs are great visual indicators that let the visitor know where they are in the site's organizational structure, while providing easy access back to higher-level pages and categories. They also provide good keyword-rich text links, providing additional relevance indicators for search engines and visitors alike.

❏ COMPATIBLE WITHOUT JAVASCRIPT

Many people browse sites without JavaScript enabled in their browsers. To ensure your site is usable by all visitors, make sure it works well without JavaScript. This doesn't mean you can't use JavaScript at all, only that visitors shouldn't be able to tell the difference without it.

❏ TEXT-ONLY COMPATIBILITY

Make sure your site can be experienced properly when images are turned off. Users still using slow connections may turn off image loading to speed up browsing. These visitors still need to be able to navigate and understand your site without those images.

❏ AVOID FLASH

While search engines can read text in flash, by its very nature, flash sites don't allow you to optimize specific landing pages effectively. For this reason, it's best to avoid all flash-based websites. Usage of small flash elements on an otherwise HTML-based web page is acceptable, provided it is not the bulk of any page.

❏ AVOID SPLASH PAGES

Splash pages are more of a hindrance to search engines and an annoyance to visitors than anything else. Let visitors get to your content quickly, avoiding any type of splash/welcome screen that adds an extra click before they reach the content they came for.

❏ ADD FAVICON

The favicon is the small image that appears to the left of your URL in the browser's address bar. Because it also appears in the browser tab when your site is open, and as the image for each page's bookmark, this small image can do a great deal of company branding. Don't leave your URL and bookmark all alone. Brand it with a custom favicon.

MOBILE-FRIENDLY DESIGN

Today, user experience on mobile is certainly getting better, because more and more sites have built mobile-optimized versions, and designers now have a better understanding of what works on the small screen. However, there's still a lot of interaction pain in doing tasks on mobile phones.[3]

–Jakob Nielsen and Raluca Budiu
Mobile Usability

WHAT THIS CHECKLIST IS ABOUT

This checklist hits on key areas to help you build a mobile-friendly website. I'll address key usability features your mobile site must have, as well as other things you can do to give your visitors a more pleasant on-site experience without sacrificing the necessities that are already a staple on the desktop version of your website.

WHY MOBILE-FRIENDLY DESIGN IS IMPORTANT

Mobile devices have turned into many people's personal assistants. So much so that it's frequently the first place people turn to when they want to research or buy a product or service. That makes mobile-friendly design a necessity in today's marketing landscape.

Search engines today produce different results based on the device on which the search is performed. Sites that are not developed with mobile usage in mind will likely not appear in search results that are performed on a smartphone or tablet.

And yet there is a distinction between sites that are mobile friendly and mobile optimized. Mobile optimized may get you in the search results, but you have to go the added step to make sure that the site is equipped for mobile usage as well. This means employing a number of user-focused design and architectural changes that ensure your visitors have a positive experience on your site when visiting from a device smartphone or tablet.

MOBILE-FRIENDLY DESIGN CHECKLIST

❏ USE RESPONSIVE OR AMP CODE

There are many routes to having a mobile site. Only two are preferred for long-term marketing value. The first is to develop your website using responsive code. Responsive websites "adjust" for every screen they are displayed on, making viewing compatible on both small and large screens. The benefit of responsive code is that you only have to update one site for all platforms. The second option is to use AMP code. AMP (Accelerated Mobile Pages) is a stripped down version of HTML designed specifically for mobile devices. This more basic version allows pages to load extremely fast. You'll want to talk to your developer about the pros and cons of using AMP for your website.

❏ DESIGNED FOR FINGERS

Fingers are fatter and far less accurate than a mouse pointer. Your mobile design needs to account for this variance. Design your buttons, links and calls to action big enough for fingertips, and with enough margin so users click what they intended, not what they didn't.

❏ COLLAPSIBLE NAVIGATION

For many sites, the navigation alone can take up an immense amount of mobile screen space. Using collapsible navigation elements, which can be opened when desired, takes the visitor right to the content without having to scroll past numerous — and unnecessary — navigational options. Be sure the button that opens your navigation is obvious so visitors can easily identify it.

❏ SHORT TEXT

Since mobile screens are smaller than desktop monitors, a little text goes a long way. A standard paragraph on your desktop display can create a lot of additional scrolling on a mobile device. It's okay to present a shortened version of your headings and content on the mobile version of your site. Provide whatever is necessary to give the visitor a quality experience, but don't be afraid to cut out anything that's not completely necessary.

❏ CHUNK CONTENT

If your on-page content can easily be broken down into sections and groups, do so. This allows visitors to avoid long pages that force them to scroll and scan just to find what they need. Content chunking allows visitors to expand or shrink each section of content to get to the information or action they desire. Look for opportunities to segment specific types of information such as ecommerce, comments, reviews and product details.

❏ LARGE FONTS

While it may seem counterintuitive to use a larger font size on a small screen, it's for that reason alone that larger fonts are necessary. Small fonts are extremely difficult to read, especially on tiny (by comparison) mobile screens. Using larger fonts makes for a better experience on your site and doesn't cause eye strain.

❏ TEXT LABEL ABOVE FIELD ENTRY

Place form field labels above each form input field, rather than on the left side. This allows for seamless vertical scroll rather than forcing the visitor to scroll left and right to read and then input into each field.

❏ PLACEHOLDER TEXT REMOVED

If you use placeholder text within any form fields, that text must disappear once the user begins to add data. Keep in mind that you should never use form field labels as placeholder text. The visitor should always be able to see the purpose of each field. When field labels are implemented as placeholder text, it's easy for the user to forget the purpose of the field.

❏ **FORM FIELD VISIBILITY**

Be sure that all form fields are visible on the page when the mobile keyboard is displayed on the screen. Check this for both portrait and landscape screens as different orientations will change the length of the page as a whole.

❏ **PRE-FILL CONTENT**

When possible, pre-fill form content based on user data. For example, let the visitor enter a zip code first so the city, state and country information can be automatically populated. The same can be done when visitors click tracking or coupon links, etc. Also, let your device pull any known information to pre-populate forms in order to make submission as easy as possible.

❏ **USE SELECTION BOXES**

Whenever possible, provide selection boxes, rather than empty fields, to help visitors fill out the forms more efficiently. Mobile users are more prone to making spelling and other mistakes when typing. Enabling pre-written selection options eliminates these mistakes.

❏ **MAKE SUGGESTIONS**

Where possible, make suggestions based on what has already been typed to complete the remaining field. This is handy when visitors routinely type in an address. If you can pull that information and auto-complete it for visitors, you've eliminated one more hurdle for them.

❏ **DON'T AUTOCORRECT EVERYTHING**

Turn off autocorrect on certain fields where various spellings are common. Names, addresses and email addresses can vary widely. Autocorrect can often cause the wrong information to be filled in without the visitor knowing.

❏ **SUPPORT COPY/PASTE**

Allow visitors to copy and paste data directly into form fields. It's frequently easier for users to find the information stored somewhere else and copy it into the form. Don't make the visitor type all the data if it's not necessary.

❏ USE CORRECT KEYBOARD

Mobile devices allow you to use different keyboards for different tasks. When someone goes to type in a phone number, don't give them the full keyboard. Instead give them just the number pad. When entering an email address, you want a keyboard with the "@" and ".com" keys readily available. Check out the various keyboards available and be sure to utilize the best one for each job.

❏ ELIMINATE POP-UPS

Eliminate all pop-ups on mobile devices. Besides getting in the way, they are often difficult to close on a small mobile screen. Mobile visitors often have to turn their screen in order to see the "X" to close these pop-ups, or they're too small to touch without hitting something else unintentionally. Help your visitors enjoy your site; eliminate those annoyances that get in the way of a good experience.

❏ ON-DEMAND SOCIAL SHARING

On desktop screens, you want your primary social sharing options to be accessible with just one click. However, on mobile devices, you want to cut down on the load time that these social sharing options require. Create a "share" call to action that opens up a social sharing menu. This falls in line with collapsible navigation and content chunking, making the mobile site more streamlined with options available upon request.

❏ UTILIZE HORIZONTAL SCROLLING

Unlike desktop web browsing, mobile phones are great for scrolling (swiping) horizontally. This provides unique advantages over the desktop web experience. Using horizontal scrolling on segmented content pieces allows you to deliver streams of information without creating long vertical scrolling pages.

❏ OPTIMIZE IMAGES

Save images in multiple sizes and resolutions so the version that is most appropriate for the screen is loaded. Many content management systems will do this automatically or have available plugins to do it for you. The goal is to display the highest resolution possible without bogging down page load time.

❏ **REDUCE HTTP REQUESTS**

Reduce the number of automated HTTP requests made when the mobile site is being downloaded. Mobile devices have less reliability when it comes to processing capabilities, bandwidth and even connection ability. Reducing the number of requests necessary to load a mobile site makes your onsite mobile experience much more reliable.

❏ **REDUCE SCRIPTS AND STYLES**

In the spirit of keeping load time to a minimum, reduce the amount of scripts and styles that are needed to run your mobile site. Each new style sheet, JavaScript or download forces the site to take longer to load and render. Keep these to a minimum for lightning-fast page loading.

❏ **CSS INSTEAD OF JAVASCRIPT**

When using animations on a mobile device, opt for CSS animations over JavaScript. CSS renders much more quickly than JavaScript and generally has fewer reliability issues.

❏ **LINK TO FULL WEBSITE**

When using separate code for the mobile and desktop versions of your site, provide a link back from the mobile version to the main desktop version. Sometimes the mobile experience doesn't provide enough information, or the visitor is just accustomed to the desktop site. By providing this link, you're ensuring that visitors won't be limited and can choose the site experience that best fits their needs.

❏ **INCREASE SPEED**

Page download speed is a major search engine ranking factor. While at some point you reach the law of diminishing returns in getting value out of increasing your site speed, you want to make sure you improve wherever you can. Keep it a priority to improve the speed at which your site loads on your visitors browsers.

SITE LOGO

In the same way that we expect to see the name of a building over the front entrances, we expect to see the Site ID at the top of the page… because the Site ID represents the whole site, which means it's the highest thing in the logical hierarchy of the site.[4]

–Steve Krug
Don't Make Me Think

WHAT THIS CHECKLIST IS ABOUT

This list covers your logo design, placement, coding, and usage on your site. While this is a relatively short checklist, each point plays a role in establishing your online presence through strong site identification.

WHY LOGOS ARE IMPORTANT

Your logo lends directly to your brand identity and website identification. It's usually the first thing your visitors see when they land on your site, and the logo serves to help them feel confident they are on a site that will meet their needs. Without an effective logo, your business name is nothing more than a word or collection of words. Even the most basic logos speak volumes about your company!

Your logo must maintain a certain level of appeal for your audience. It helps immediately establish your credibility and professionalism, while also helping to set the tone for what visitors will experience on your site. Your logo should give the visitors a sense of *who* you are while also identifying *what* you do.

On your site, your logo must fulfill very specific roles to ensure you have proper website usability measures implemented. The placement of your logo, how it's linked and what it says all serve the purpose to enhance or detract from your visitors' experience on your website.

A good logo, along with good design, gives your visitors an element of confidence in your company. It also helps you stand out from your competitors and gives your visitors a means for remembering you. In short, a logo is (or should be) memorable.

SITE LOGO CHECKLIST

❏ UNIQUE AND ORIGINAL

Above all else, your logo needs to be unique and original to you and you alone. While some design elements are similar between logos, be sure to avoid any appearance of similarity between yours and a competitor's. Let your logo help you stand out and be unique.

❏ STANDS OUT ON THE WEBSITE

The logo itself should stand out on the website. Use plenty of white space around the logo to avoid any other design elements encroaching into its territory. The logo should be clear and distinctive from the other top navigational elements, not blending into the background in any way. Make it as distinctive as possible, fitting for the design of your site.

❏ DISPLAYS COMPANY NAME CLEARLY

The most important element of your logo is your company name. Designs, icons and taglines are all valuable; however, nothing should distract the visitor from clearly and visibly registering your company name. Keep your logo minimalistic, eliminating unnecessary eye candy so your name remains unobstructed and the visitor undistracted.

❏ POSITIONED TOP-LEFT

You should almost always place your logo at the top-left of each page of your site. Most visitors intuitively and immediately look to the top-left of the page for immediate site identification. When you put your logo in any other location, including only a few pixels to the top-center, you break expectations, and not in a good way.

❏ INCORPORATES TAGLINE

Your tagline does not necessarily need to be part of your logo, but the two go hand-in-hand. Use your tagline consistently across the site, located near the logo itself. As with the logo, the tagline needs to have plenty of white space from other design elements to ensure it maintains strong visibility.

❏ LINKS TO HOME PAGE

Many web users instinctively click on a site's logo when they want to navigate back to the home page. Even if you have a "Home" navigational link, linking the logo ensures that visitors can quickly get where they want to go with minimal searching. Not linking your logo to your home page forces visitors to find the alternate navigational links, delaying them from getting to that page.

❏ SCHEMA LOGO MARKUP

Use schema.org logo markup to provide the search engines with the canonical version of your home page URL. Schema markup also provides a signal to the search engines so they know what image they should display in search results and/or knowledge graph when brand searches are performed.

Example

```
<div itemscope itemtype="http://schema.org/Organization">
    <a itemprop="url" href="http://www.site.com/">Home</a>
    <img itemprop="logo" src="http://www.site.com/logo.png" />
</div>
```

❏ CREATE A FAVICON

Favicons are like your website's official avatar. Whenever someone visits or bookmarks a page on your site, the favicon acts as a small branding mechanism that is displayed in the browser's location bar and also as the bookmark icon. You can use this to passively build brand recognition for your site and to help visitors find your open page when they have multiple browser tabs open.

SITE ARCHITECTURE ISSUES

The right site structure can help your SEO efforts flourish while the wrong one can cripple them.[5]

–Danny Sullivan
Third Door Media

WHAT THIS CHECKLIST IS ABOUT

This checklist covers important website architectural issues that can have an impact on your website's ability to attract, engage and convert visitors, as well as obtain important search engine rankings. While this list does not cover ongoing optimization factors, the "how-to" of SEO, or any detailed optimization strategies, the items here will help you create a more search engine-friendly website that can be indexed, analyzed and ranked for relevant searches.

WHY SITE ARCHITECTURE IS IMPORTANT

The backend architecture of your site can make or break your website's performance in the search engines. In all, site architecture can account for about 30% of a successful SEO campaign and easily account for 100% of a website's lack of performance.

Without a solid site architecture, and proper architectural implementation, your website can end up with a number of performance-killing stumbling blocks that will affect your visitor's experience on your website, and/or prevent the search engines from ranking your content where it deserves. You'll find yourself with fewer indexed pages, lower rankings, less visitors and lackluster sales.

A number of architectural issues can be overlooked by the search engines as they get better at analyzing and interpreting web code. However, I've never been a big fan of leaving it to the search engines to interpret a site correctly. Interpretation leaves room for mistakes, and those mistakes can cost a great deal when you're not being found in the search results. The best solution is a permanent fix for whatever problems are affecting your website.

Properly implemented site architecture fixes a number of impediments, paving the way for a website that functions optimally on all levels. Good architecture creates a more visitor- and search engine-friendly website that will boost crawlability, improve navigation, create better search relevance and increase conversion rates.

SITE ARCHITECTURE CHECKLIST

❏ FULLY HTTPS/SSL SECURE

In the past, businesses only cared about making sure their shopping carts and forms were using HTTPS for security. With the growing push toward security, it is now wise to move your entire site to HTTPS by purchasing an SSL Digital Certificate for your domain name. You'll need to work with your web host to ensure all your URLs are now running HTTPS, and that the HTTP versions of your URLs are properly 301 redirecting to the HTTPS version. Not only is this a good idea for security, search engines have also made HTTPS/SSL a ranking factor that can give your site a (small) boost over non-secure competitors.

❏ ADD HREFLANG ATTRIBUTE

The hreflang attribute is used to indicate the language used on each page of your site. This is especially important if you use multiple languages and dialects on your website to target visitors in other countries.

Example:
```
<link rel="alternate" href="http://example.com"
     hreflang="en-us" />
```

❏ KEEP SECURITY CERTIFICATE CURRENT

Be sure to keep your site security certificate up to date. Any lapse in this can disrupt the sales process and call your entire site's security into question. Even a temporary issue here can cause you to lose customers for life.

❏ CORRECT ROBOTS.TXT FILE

When search engines visit your site, they download the robots.txt file to know which pages they should and should not crawl and index. A simple error in this file can prevent search engines from accessing important pages, or the entire site can be blocked completely. Review your robots.txt file for correct formatting to ensure you're only blocking those pages you don't want included in the search results.

❏ DECLARE DOCTYPE

The doctype declaration in each page's head tag tells the browsers how to read and render the code that was used to create the page. Without a declared doctype, the browser (and search engine) may read your site very differently than intended. This can lead to problems with how the page displays, as well as potential issues with the search engines, and their algorithmic interpretation of each page.

Example
```
<DOCTYPE html>
```

❏ VALIDATE HTML

HTML validation has little to do with improving a site's performance, but poorly constructed and invalidated HTML can create some very troublesome issues. To ensure your site has no performance-crippling HTML problems, run your pages through an HTML validation tool and fix as many of the issues as you can. You don't have to have 100% compliant code, but eliminate as many errors as possible throughout the site to ensure there is nothing creating performance drag.

❏ VALIDATE CSS

Confirm that your CSS validates (as much as possible) to ensure proper rendering of your styles on all browsers. Malformed CSS can produce unwanted visual errors when the site is being viewed.

❏ SPIDERABLE CSS AND JAVASCRIPT

Don't hide your CSS and JavaScript files from the search engines. As more information is being moved off-page into CSS and JavaScript, search engines need to read these files in order to properly understand the context of each page. Hiding this information can ultimately harm your search engine marketing efforts.

❏ DON'T USE HTML FRAMES

Frames are an old-school method of incorporating multiple pages of content into a single page. Newer and more search engine-friendly technologies are available that do the same thing, only better, for both visitors and search engines. If your site still uses frames, it's time for an upgrade.

❏ USE ALT ATTRIBUTE ON ALL IMAGES

Alternative (alt) text can be added to any image that will be used by both search engines and visitors alike. Alt text allows the search engines to have a better understanding of what the image is, which then plays a role in image search. Visitors with images turned off see the alt text instead of the image, providing them with a greater understanding of what the image is there for. Every image on your site should include an alt attribute with properly descriptive text.

Example
```
<img src=" site.com/image.png" alt="description of
     image"/>
```

❏ 404 BAD URLS

If a bad or broken link that you are unaware of is accessed by a visitor, leading to a URL that does not exist, be sure that the URL produces a 404 notice. This notice tells the search engines that this is not a valid URL to be spidered, and it will also lead visitors to content that tells them the page they are looking for is not at that URL.

❏ REDIRECT OLD URLS

Any page that has changed URLs should not produce a 404 notice for the old URL, but rather there should be an automatic redirect to the new URL. This ensures your visitors find the content they need quicker and the search engines know to pass all the established value of the old URL to the new one. There are two primary redirects, 301 (permanent) and 302 (temporary.) Be sure to implement the most appropriate one.

❏ PRINTER-FRIENDLY CSS

Use CSS to create printer-friendly pages, rather than creating separate URLs for printing. Printer-friendly CSS can produce a page perfectly designed for output on printed paper, without unneeded navigation links— which can't be "clicked" on a printed page anyway. It also eliminates duplicate content that "printer-friendly" URLs cause.

❏ UNDERLINE CLICKABLE LINKS

In the early days of the web, all clickable links were blue and underlined. Since then, many sites have used different color links to fit the color scheme of the site, but underlining has become a universal indicator that the text is a link that can be clicked. Links that are not underlined (except navigation links) tend to get overlooked by the visitor who doesn't realize that the otherwise-styled text is an action element. Underlining all links by default ensures visitors know what it is and what to do.

Examples
No: *Always underline link text in your content.*
Yes: *Always <u>underline link text</u> in your content.*

❏ DIFFERING LINK TEXT STYLES

Any linked text in standard text areas should appear differently than the rest of the text. Traditionally, this text has been blue; however, it is now common and acceptable to change the link style elements (such as color, bold or italics) to fit your preference. The one caveat to this is that the link must remain underlined as noted above, as this is the universal "link" indicator. In all, linked text must stand out from other textual elements.

Examples
No: *Always **underline link text** in your content.*
Yes: *Always **<u>underline link text</u>** in your content.*

No: *Always underline link text in your content.*
Yes: *Always <u>underline link text</u> in your content.*

❏ CANONICAL BREADCRUMB URLS

When incorporating breadcrumbs that follow the navigation path of the visitor, be sure to maintain consistent URL usage throughout the site. Don't allow the breadcrumb trail to create different URLs that produce the same content on the page.

For example, if a visitor travels from *Home > Books > Gardening > Book Title* or *Home > Gardening > Books > Book Title*, the end URL should be exactly the same, not breadcrumb trail specific. Also, be sure to use proper schema markup for your breadcrumb trail.

❏ PROPER PAGE HIERARCHY

Your pages should be laid out within an established hierarchal format using categories and sub-categories appropriately. Cross-link pages within their own categories consistently, and avoid mass linking to non-related category sub-pages. This helps produce a hierarchal flow for search engines to follow and allows them to understand how pages are related to each other.

❏ BALANCED DIRECTORY STRUCTURE

When establishing your navigation and site directory structure, keep a balance between a directory structure that is either too flat or too deep. It's best if visitors and search engines can get to each page without too much clicking, while still providing them some topical relevance within the link hierarchy.

A flat navigation is just as bad as a deep navigation. When all pages are in the site's root folder or only one click away from the home page, there isn't enough context categorization in place. This categorization is beneficial for both visitors and search engines to see more about a page's topical context within the site.

With the exception of very large sites, each page should be accessible within five clicks of the home page, with two to three clicks being optimal.

❏ UNIQUE TITLE TAGS

Each page should have a unique title tag that is not duplicated on any other page. This title should reflect the content of the specific page, providing unique value to the reader. When dealing with pagination of products (or blog posts) of the same category, simply adding "page 2," "page 3," etc., to the title can be sufficient in ensuring each title tag is unique.

Title tags should be no more than 65 characters in length in order to keep them from being cut short in the search results.

Example
```
<title>Page Title Goes Here, Use Up to 65 Characters</
    title>
```

❏ Unique Meta Descriptions

As with the title tag, each page should include a unique meta description that accurately summarizes the content of the page. Since the meta description is not used as a ranking factor, you can incorporate value/benefit-oriented language as a means to persuade searchers to click into your site. The meta description should be no more than 150 characters in length to ensure it does not get truncated in search results.

Example
```
<meta name="description" content="Meta description
content information goes here. You have up to 150 or
so characters. Use them!"/>
```

❏ Properly Bulleted Lists

Use <ol>, <ul> and <li> HTML markup to designate bulleted lists. When bulleted lists are coded as standard text, the search engines have no way to interpret them properly, and therefore cannot assign appropriate value to the text. Using proper markup ensures search engines read the content the way it is intended to be read.

Examples
Bulleted List:
```
<ul>
    <li>Bullet one</li>
    <li>Bullet two</li>
    <li>Bullet three</li>
</ul>
```

Numbered List:
```
<ol>
    <li>Number 1</li>
    <li>Number 2</li>
    <li>Number 3</li>
</ol>
```

❏ ELIMINATE CODE BLOAT

Modern HTML and CSS allow you to develop your pages with very minimal on-page code. This reduces the amount of code the visitor and search engines must download to render the site, therefore speeding up the time it takes to access each page. Eliminate as much bloated code as you can. You want to keep your pages lean and fast for visitors and search engines alike.

❏ REDUCE TABLE USAGE

HTML tables are great for organizing on-page content, but they also produce a lot of unnecessary code. This can slow down the browser's rendering of your page and increase page download times. Whenever possible, use CSS to create table-styled content rather than using bloated HTML tables.

❏ ABSOLUTE LINKS IN NAVIGATION

While relative links are easier to work with when a site is in development, using absolute URLs in your site's navigation can eliminate many potential issues later on. Absolute links are not subject to interpretation like relative links, and tell the visitor and search engine the exact URL intended.

Examples
Relative link: `<a href="/page.html">`
Absolute link: `<a href="http://www.site.com/page.html">`

❏ NON-SPIDERABLE SHOPPING CART LINKS

Any links pointed to your shopping cart (add to cart, view cart, checkout, etc.) should not be spiderable for the search engines. These are areas of the site the search engines don't need to index. Making the links completely hidden from the search engines prevents them from being followed or having them factored into the algorithms.

❏ "DISALLOW" PAGES FOR NO SEARCH ENGINE EVALUATION

Use the robots.txt file to prevent the search engines from accessing any specific pages or sections of the site that you don't want them to crawl. URLs disallowed in the robots.txt file can still show up in search results, but the content of the page won't be used when the search engine is evaluating the page. Keep in mind, when using this tag, search engines will not see any other directives that may be in the code of the disallowed page.

Examples
Disallow: `/disallowed-directory/`
Disallow: `/indexed-directory/disallowed-page.html`

❏ "NOINDEX" PAGES TO NOT SHOW IN SERPS

Use the robots meta tag in the code of a page to prevent the search engines from indexing that page and to keep it completely out of the search results. NoIndexed pages can continue to pass value to other pages via links, but the URLs will not show up in the search results, nor will the content be analyzed. Blog category and tag pages are good examples of pages you might want to NoIndex, since those are merely pages that link to actual blog posts.

Examples
```
<meta name="robots" content="noindex, nofollow">
<meta name="robots" content="noindex, follow">
```

Note: The "follow" attribute tells the search engines whether you would like them to follow the links that lead off the page. Generally, it's a good idea unless those links go to pages you don't want indexed.

❏ "NOFOLLOW" LINKS TO PREVENT PASSING VALUE

If you have links to any internal or external pages that you do not want to pass link value, use a NoFollow attribute within the link code. The search engines may still follow the link at their discretion, but this attribute will prevent the link from passing value to the destination page. The destination page may still obtain link value from other links on the web, but not from any links with the NoFollow attribute.

Example
```
<a href="http://www.site.com/page.html"
rel="nofollow"> NoFollowed Link</a>
```

❏ CHECK FOR BROKEN LINKS

Regularly perform a broken link check on your site and fix any links to URLs that are no longer valid, whether internal or external. Sites with an inordinate amount of broken links can appear unmaintained, potentially losing some "authority" points with the search engines. Blogs are especially susceptible to having broken links as they are more likely to link to external sites that become obsolete and removed from the web over time. Keep all links directed at existing pages and remove or fix the links that do not.

❏ INCREASE PAGE DOWNLOAD SPEED

Slow-loading pages frustrate visitors and can have a negative impact on your search engine rankings. Look for opportunities to speed up page load times so you don't annoy your visitors with slow-loading pages, or give search engines a reason to lower your site's authority value.

❏ REDUCE LINKS ON PAGE

Every link out to another page reduces the "link value" you keep on the linking page. Reduce the number of outbound links on each page of your site in order to maintain as much link value as possible on each page. There are some valid exceptions to this rule (product category pages, etc.,) but minimizing outbound links is always a good rule to follow. With that said, don't be stingy either. If there is a valid reason to link, do it.

Whenever possible, the maximum number of links on a page should be kept to 100 or less. Staying well below this number is even better. Streamline your navigation so you have room to include additional text links in content areas.

❏ AVOID DUPLICATE CONTENT

Don't allow multiple URLs to display the same or very similar content to each other. Each URL should produce unique content that cannot be found elsewhere on your site (or the web, for that matter). When using URL parameters, be sure that each parameter allows for unique content to be displayed on the page.

❏ USE PROPER HEADING TAG HIERARCHY

Structure your heading tags so each page has one unique H1 tag and the H2-4 tags are used for content purposes only. If heading tags are required for page structure outside of the content, stick to using H5-6 tags for this. All textual heading tags should be used in a proper hierarchal format, with the H1 being the highest and most important.

Examples
```
<h1>The Page's Most Important Headline, Usually at the
Top</h1>
    <h2>Can Be Used as a Sub-Headline or for Second-
    Most Important Paragraph Heading</h2>
        <h3>Third Most Important Heading for Breaking Up
        Content</h3>
```

❏ AVOID SESSION IDs

Don't use session IDs to track visitor usage on your web pages. Session IDs append a tracking code to the end of the URL for each visitor, essentially creating a unique URL for every page each visitor sees. This creates severe duplicate content issues and causes you to split valuable link and social juice between different URLs with the exact same content.

Examples
Visitor 1:   *site.com/page1.html?ID=123456*
Visitor 2:   *site.com/page1.html?ID=789123*
Visitor 3:   *site.com/page1.html?ID=456789*

❏ SEARCH ENGINE-FRIENDLY LINKS

All internal site links should use proper HTML coding, rather than JavaScript or other questionable coding. Only pure HTML coded links are assured to be followable by the search engines with proper link value being passed. Unless you deliberately want to prevent links from passing value (such as to shopping cart pages), code them using proper HTML.

Example
```
No:  <a href="javascript:void(0)"
     onclick="myJsFunc();">
Yes: <a href="http://www.site.com/page.html">
```

❏ USE STRUCTURED DATA

Incorporate schema.org structured data into your site's code. Search engines use this data to better understand key elements of your site, which translates into better interpretation for ranking value, as well as shows how these elements might display in search results. Review all relevant structured data for ecommerce, mobile, local and general architecture.

CONVERSION OPTIMIZATION & USABILITY ISSUES

As a rule, conventions (best practices) only become conventions if they work. Well-applied conventions make it easier for users to go from site to site without expending a lot of effort figuring out how things work.[6]

–Steve Krug
Don't Make Me Think

WHAT THIS CHECKLIST IS ABOUT

This checklist covers conversion "best practices" that have been developed and refined as the web has evolved throughout the last two decades. Each point here is useful in helping you understand what visitors expect to find on your site and to create an experience that makes it easier for visitors to achieve their (and your) goals, without losing any of your uniqueness.

WHY CONVERSION OPTIMIZATION AND USABILITY IS IMPORTANT

Most usability problems go unnoticed by the average web user, at least on a conscious level. Heck, many visitors may tell you just how great your site is, even while it's rife with problems! Despite the accolades, your site is very likely underperforming in getting the coveted conversions you want. Fixing usability issues isn't about getting more pats on the back for your awesome website; it's about creating the best user experience possible for every visitor on your site.

Many things done by web developers can look good to the eye but can just as often be annoying to the typical visitor. It might be obvious, such as content that is hard to read or call to action buttons that are hard to find. However, most usability issues are usually less obvious and would never even be noticed by visitors. It's more of a hidden stumbling block than an obvious one. Kind of like an annoying sound that bothers you for 10 minutes before you realize you even hear it.

Many sites perform just fine, but they are unknowingly losing a lot of conversions due to usability issues that are annoying visitors. The following action points may not fix every problem on your site, and some may not work at all, but by testing each usability change you make, you can know which ones produce the best gains and which to ignore completely. Hopefully in the process you'll uncover new issues to test as well.

Finding and fixing usability issues on your site will make it easier for your visitors to stay engaged with your content. The less frustrated visitors are, the easier they get what they need, and the more you'll see each visitor "converting" into a customer.

CONVERSION OPTIMIZATION & USABILITY CHECKLIST

❏ WHAT'S IMPORTANT IS PROMINENT

Make sure that the most important pieces of content or on-page elements are the most prominent on the page. You can do this through some combination of being bigger, bolder, in a distinctive color, set off by more white space, or placed in a more noticeable area of the page. Don't bury your important content, but let visitors see and interact with it as needed.

❏ VISUALLY RELATE LOGICAL ELEMENTS

Things that are related logically should also be related visually as well. Show their similarity by grouping them together under a heading, displaying them in a similar visual style, or putting them all in a clearly defined area of the page.

❏ CLEARLY DEFINED PAGE AREAS

Break up your pages into clearly defined areas. Users should be able to tell exactly what each section of the page is about. This allows them to quickly decide which areas of the page to focus on based on their interest, and which areas they can safely ignore.

❏ HIGH-DEFINITION IMAGES

Images are how you dress up your site. If you're using low quality images, then you risk being under-dressed for the customer, giving a perception of low caliber service or products. Always use high definition images throughout your site.

❏ CLICKABLE ELEMENTS ARE OBVIOUS

Make clickable elements recognizable. Visitors are always looking for the next thing to move on to, and by clearly marking clickable elements, you are presenting them with the opportunity to stay engaged with your content. Don't squander the limited patience that each visitor brings to a new site, but keep them moving through your site by providing access to the information they need. This keeps them more fully engaged in the conversion process.

❏ MINIMIZE NOISE

Too much busyness or "background" on the page can create "noise" that distracts the visitor from properly interacting with your site. Busyness is when there are too many things all clamoring for the visitor's attention. Background is small bits of visual noise that mentally wears the visitor down. Eliminating such noise gives the visitor a more "comfortable" environment in which to properly interact with your site.

❏ OMIT NEEDLESS WORDS

There are two types of writing styles that you must be careful with: happy talk and instructions. Happy talk is text that has no real value to the visitor and acts as a barrier that stands in the way of the visitor getting to the real content meat. Cut out this useless happy talk so visitors can get to what is important.

Instructions almost always go unread by the visitor as they move right on to the task they set out to do. Make any steps as self-explanatory as possible so no lengthy instructions are needed.

❏ CONSISTENT NAVIGATION PLACEMENT

Make sure your global navigation is in the same place and works the same way on every page. Don't change your main navigation from page to page as this confuses visitors and forces them to have to "figure out" how to navigate with each change. Consistent navigation makes site navigation easy and seamless for the visitor.

❏ INCORPORATE ON-SITE SEARCH

Give your users a way to search your site. When they reach a new site, a large percentage of visitors immediately look for a search box that allows them to find the content they need. Incorporate a simple site search option: a box, a button and the word "search." Avoid fancy wording and instructions; keep it simple and effective.

❏ HIGHLIGHT CURRENT LOCATION

Highlight the visitor's current location on your site in your navigational bars with at least two visual elements. You can do things as simple as placing a pointer (or arrow) next to the navigation link that reflects the currently viewed page, change the text color, use bold text, reverse the button or change background colors. Use one or more of these options to make it clear to the visitor what page and/or section of the site they are viewing.

❏ CONTRAST CALLS TO ACTION

When visitors are engaging with your site, you want it to be obvious what action they should take next. Make sure the main call to action on each page contrasts with the other on-page visual elements. Use design elements such as color, size and font to set your calls to action apart.

❏ ESTABLISH TRUST AND CREDIBILITY

Make sure you give your site visitors something that makes them confident in doing business with you. Display symbols for awards, memberships and personal information protection that help communicate your business's legitimacy. Also, a robust about us page can give your visitors many additional security signals they need.

❏ VISUALLY CONNECTED TAGLINE

Create a tagline that is visually connected to your site ID (logo). This is a short phrase that sums up what you do and what makes your business great. Your tagline should communicate a clear difference between you and your competitors, while also providing at least one benefit of doing business with you.

❏ DON'T OVER-PROMOTE

Don't try to highlight everything you do on the home page. Too many options or too much information on the home page can have a negative impact on visitors achieving the goals of your site. Your home page should help users navigate the most common tasks and important elements only.

❏ DON'T HIDE NEEDED INFO

Customers want stuff like phone numbers, shipping rates and prices, among other bits of information. Make sure important information such as this is readily available. It may cost you some money and additional time to make it all viewable, but the net gain received often over-compensates for whatever you thought it would cost you to make it happen.

❏ FLEXIBLE FORM INPUTS

Don't punish your visitors for not doing things your way. Site visitors should never have to think about how to properly format data they are entering into forms. Make sure all input labels are clear and very little thought is required. Let them enter it their way and you can work out the rest.

❏ REQUEST ONLY NECESSARY INFO

Don't ask for information you don't really need. Visitors are already skeptical, and it is annoying when sites request information they know isn't really essential. Stick to requiring only that information that is necessary for the task at hand.

❏ EASY TO USE

What are the main things that your visitors want to do or should do on your site? Figure out the three main things they will want to accomplish and make sure these are the top priority actions available for them. Make them obvious and easy to do.

❏ **TELL VISITORS WHAT THEY WANT TO KNOW**

Don't hide important information in small print or on hard-to-find pages. Be upfront, even if the information is considered "negative." You'll often gain trust points for candor and honesty by bringing this information to the forefront, rather than the visitor being surprised by it later.

❏ **REDUCE STEPS TO GOAL COMPLETION**

Once the visitor starts down a path to complete a goal, minimize the number of steps in the process. For example, instead of giving your visitors a shipment tracking number that requires them to find the carrier website and then enter the tracking number, provide them with a link that takes them directly to their shipment tracking information. Visitors will appreciate even the smallest things you do to make engagement with your site easier.

❏ **ANSWER RELEVANT QUESTIONS**

Make sure your Frequently Asked Questions are really that. FAQ pages should not be full of questions you wish visitors would ask. Give your visitors answers to what *they* want to know, not just what you want them to know.

❏ **LIVE CHAT**

Give shoppers an option to chat with a representative in real time. When shoppers are hesitant to buy a product, a quick chat session can help them get all their questions answered and proceed to the purchase.

❏ **EASY ERROR RECOVERY**

Form submission errors are unavoidable. Forcing the visitor to refill all their data is not. When a form submission error happens, always maintain the previously entered data so the visitor can quickly fix the error and move on.

❏ **ALWAYS BE TESTING**

Because of business and customer complexity, the only "best practices" that exist are the ones that have been discovered through knowing your business and understanding your specific audience. Testing all of the elements in this checklist is the only way to uncover the real best practices for your website.

SITE NAVIGATION

The design of a website's navigation has a bigger impact on success or failure than almost any other factor. It affects traffic and search engine rankings. It affects conversions and user-friendliness. *Everything important about your website is connected to the navigation*, from content to the URLs.[7]

–Andy Crestodina
Orbit Media Studios

WHAT THIS CHECKLIST IS ABOUT

This list covers issues regarding your site's navigational elements, including primary, secondary, and sub-navigation. It provides tips on how to make your navigation both effective for search engines and friendly for visitors at the same time.

WHY SITE NAVIGATION IS IMPORTANT

When on your website, your navigation is the primary way visitors are able to locate the information that is most relevant to their needs. While good optimization will bring visitors to the page that best reflects their desire, there is always a need for a strong user and search engine-friendly navigation. This helps both visitors and search engine spiders navigate through your site to find valuable information.

Your site's navigation alone can give your visitors a very strong indication of the products or services that you offer, and it acts as the guide for getting them to that content. The goal is to get your visitors the information they need with as few hurdles as possible, so they can get what they came for and move on quickly and easily.

The more hunting each visitor has to do in order to find what they need, the more likely they are to get frustrated on your site. At the same time, if you overload your visitors with too many options, they can become confused as to which option will give them the information they came for. A balance must be struck between too many and too few navigational options. A proper navigation maintains that balance, ensuring the visitors get to the information they want, quickly.

For the search engine, the goals are similar. Too many options mean little or no site hierarchal development that the search engines use in valuing pages and ranking content. But you have to make sure the search engines can get to any page with as few jumps (clicks) as possible.

When your site's navigation is broken, or isn't optimized for search and visitors, you'll see abandonment rates higher than what they should be. This can result in less search engine traffic and less business overall. An optimized site navigation will serve both the visitor and the engine to ensure both are able to get what they need and interact with the site in the most optimal way.

SITE NAVIGATION CHECKLIST

❏ PRIMARY NAV LOCATED TOP-LEFT

Navigational elements are traditionally located at the top and/or left side of the page. Placing your navigation anywhere else forces your visitors to search the page just to know what navigational options are available. While there are always legitimate exceptions to the top/left rule, use caution when going outside of your visitor's expectations.

❏ SITE-WIDE CONSISTENCY

As with most elements on each page of your site, maintain consistency of placement, colors, size, etc. Every change to "static" navigational elements takes the visitor away from the content, which is where they are most likely to maintain engagement with all that you have to offer.

❑ EASY TO USE

Don't make visitors think too much in order to use your site's navigation. Simplicity of use requires keyword-rich navigational headings and links, non-frustrating drop-down or fly-out elements (an oxymoron, if you ask me) and limiting the number of navigational options. Each link should be clear in meaning and obvious as to what content will be available once it's clicked.

❑ HTML LINKS

All navigation links must be HTML based rather than JavaScript or Flash. While search engines are getting better at reading that type of content, only HTML-based links are guaranteed to be read, followed and link value properly attributed by search engines.

❑ LINK TO MAIN SITE SECTIONS

If your site's services or offerings are broken down into categories, display those categories as your main navigational elements. While other areas of the site might be important, it's assumed that your products and services are most important of all. Don't force visitors to click on "services" or "products" just to see what you offer. Instead, present these as the core of your visible navigation. You may have to narrow down or group your offerings into fewer options, but this all goes toward creating a simple navigation that improves the visitor's experience on your site.

❑ LINK TO KEY COMPANY PAGES

Aside from your main offerings, your navigation must also help your visitors find key company information to assist them in the decision-making process of choosing to do business with you over a competitor. There are a number of pages you can add to your main, visible navigation, but only a handful that are absolutely necessary. All non-essential pages can often be grouped under navigational sub-categories.

Here are some of the links that you may want visible in the main navigation:

❑ HOME PAGE   ❑ BLOG
❑ CONTACT US PAGE   ❑ LOGIN/LOGOUT
❑ ABOUT US PAGE   ❑ SHOPPING CART

❏ PROPER CATEGORICAL DIVISIONS

When using a large side-navigation with many links, be sure to break the links into categorical groups rather than showing one long list. This helps visitors quickly scan and focus on an area of the navigation that best represents their needs and wants.

❏ ACCURATE LINK TEXT

The text used in each navigation link should accurately (and very succinctly) describe the destination page. You usually have space for one to three words, depending on the navigation format you use. Incorporate descriptive keywords that ensure the visitor doesn't have to guess what they will find on the destination page once they click the link.

❏ NO INDUSTRY JARGON

The text used in your navigation links should be easy to understand by all users — those familiar with your industry and those who are not. Don't use industry jargon in your links, or use acronyms that may not be understood by non-industry folk. Use language that each visitor will instinctively understand and that hints to the content they will find on the destination page.

❏ DROP-DOWN HEADINGS CLICKABLE

Many navigations use a mouse-over effect to trigger a drop down that opens up more navigation choices. Quite often, the mouse-over headers are not clickable links that lead to another page. They should be. Anything that looks and acts like a navigation link should lead visitors to a working page. Navigation elements that don't "work" feel broken. Besides, these pages can often serve as great optimized landing pages for general category keywords.

❏ OBVIOUS NON-CLICKABLE ELEMENTS

Any header-type navigation element that isn't an actual clickable link should appear obviously different from the other clickable elements in the navigation. If it looks like a clickable link, the visitor will try to click it, only to get frustrated when it doesn't work.

❏ LINKS ARE VISUALLY OBVIOUS

Don't require visitors to rely on their mouse pointer to tell them what is or isn't a link. All links, navigational and contextual, should be visually different from other text on the site.

❏ MOUSE POINTER CHANGES ON CLICKABLE LINKS

Many sites use navigation coding that doesn't change the mouse pointer to the "pointing finger" icon when it hovers over a link. This icon is the tell-tale signal that something is an actual clickable link. Code your navigation so that all clickable elements change the mouse pointer to the proper icon, so visitors know what is or isn't clickable.

❏ CURRENT PAGE IDENTIFICATION

While breadcrumbs help visitors see where they are in the current navigational trail, it is also helpful for visitors to see which page they are on when looking at their navigational options. This can be done by creating a slight color or other visual change on the link for the page currently being viewed. This visual cue can be a subtle but effective means of helping visitors keep track of where they are in your site.

❏ IMAGE LINKS USE ALT TEXT

You generally want to avoid using images as your main navigation; however, there are times when images in your navigation can provide a visual assist for visitors. When such images are used, be sure to use alt text in the image code that describes the navigation link.

Example

```
<img src="site.com/services.png" alt="Our Services"/>
```

❏ Use Absolute Links

Absolute links create a hard-coded URL to the destination page that leaves little room for browser or search engine misinterpretation. When relative links are used, problems can occur that can cause the browser and the search engines to interpret the link incorrectly, resulting in the link being broken. Use absolute links to prevent such errors.

Examples
Absolute link: `<a href="http://www.site.com/page.html">`
Relative link: `<a href="/page.html">`

❏ Internal Links Open in Same Window/Tab

Primary navigation links should almost always open the destination page in the current window or tab being used by the visitor. When navigation links open in a new window or tab, the visitor loses the fluid navigational experience and they cannot use their "back" button. If the visitor spends enough time navigating around your site, they'll end up with numerous open tabs and windows. That's just annoying!

❏ External Links Open in New Window/Tab

While not absolutely necessary, it's a good idea to have any link that points to an external site open in a new window or tab. When visitors follow links off your site, they often wish to get back to the page of your site they left. Opening external links in a new window/tab allows them to quickly get back to your site without having to hit the back button repeatedly.

❏ No Flyout Menus

Drop down menus can make navigating to sub-categories easier. However, flyout menus (sub-navigation links that slide out to the right or left) are often very difficult to use. All too often, visitors are unable to keep the mouse perfectly in line with the flyout, causing it to close before they are able to click the next link. Flyouts are great if you have perfect mousing skills, but otherwise, not so much. However, if you choose to use flyout menus, adjust the timing so when the mouse accidentally moves off the menu item, the flyout menu won't close prematurely.

❑ SIMPLE FOOTER

Keep your footer as simple as possible. Footer navigation links should be kept to a minimum, providing links to pages that are important but not fitting for the main (upper) navigational areas of the site.

Some typical footer links might include:

❑ **SITEMAP**   ❑ **PROMOTIONAL MATERIALS**
❑ **PRIVACY POLICY** ❑ **SOCIAL LINKS**
❑ **SECURITY SIGNALS** ❑ **ACCREDITATIONS AND ORGANIZATIONS**

❑ NO "SITEMAP" NAVIGATION

Your primary or footer navigation should never act as a sitemap for your entire site, unless your site is extremely light on pages (25 or less). While it's important to give your visitors multiple options that help them reach their destination, a sitemap-style navigation creates too many options for the visitor, making it harder — not easier — for them to find what they are looking for.

❑ ADD A SITEMAP

While most visitors can, and will, use your navigation sufficiently, there are always times when the easiest way to find something is to go to a sitemap page. Create an HTML sitemap that allows visitors to quickly find the information they need, without hunting through multiple navigational layers and clicks.

❑ USE BREADCRUMBS

Breadcrumbs are an important ingredient to a complete site navigation structure. Breadcrumbs help visitors move back one or more categories with just a single click, instead of being forced to hunt for the category link in the navigation menu. Breadcrumbs also provide the visitor with visual cues as to where they are in your site, while also allowing them to navigate around a category more easily.

Examples
Home > About PPM > Stoney deGeyter
Home > Library > eBooks > The Best Damn Web Marketing Cheat Sheet!

INTERNAL SITE SEARCH

> SSA [Site Search Analytics] provides an unmatched trove of semantic richness — not just what users want, but the tone and flavor of the language they use to express those needs. And it's without the biases introduced by testing and a lab environment.[8]
>
> –Louis Rosenfeld
> *Search Analytics for Your Site*

WHAT THIS CHECKLIST IS ABOUT

Effective on-site search is more than simply integrating a search box into your site's navigation. Both the placement of the search box and how the results are displayed can make your site search either a boon or a bust for your visitors. This checklist helps you craft a site search function that enhances your user experience by getting them to the content they want quickly and effectively.

WHY INTERNAL SITE SEARCH IS IMPORTANT

On-site search is an important option in creating a more robust user experience on your website. While your navigation should be streamlined to help visitors find things as quickly as possible, when visitors don't know how to use the navigation to find specific information, they turn to site search.

Having an effective site search feature gives visitors a way to get to very specific information quickly, avoiding having to go through your primary navigation, jumping through multiple levels and options, just hoping to find what they need. It allows them to find what they want without forcing them into a multi-click navigational maze, searching for something they don't know how to find.

The data you get from site searches can also give you a wealth of information as to what your visitors typically want when on your site. This can help you highlight certain products or information on your home page, craft special offers or even determine which pages would benefit from additional optimization.

In any case, site search can be used proactively and reactively to enhance the visitor's experience on the site. It doesn't replace your navigation, but it is a necessary supplement to an already well-crafted navigational structure.

INTERNAL SITE SEARCH CHECKLIST

❏ LOCATE IN TOP-RIGHT CORNER

You can put your site search anywhere, but the most common place is in the top-right corner of the page. While this may change as websites evolve, you generally want your site search to be where visitors are most accustomed to finding it. Until proven otherwise (by testing on your site), place your site search in the top-right corner.

❏ LABEL AS "SEARCH"

Your search box should be labeled properly so visitors immediately know its purpose. The word "search" is critical, though a short message can be included such as "search products" or "search blog," etc. You can add this label either above, beside, in the search field, or the search button itself.

❏ LINK TO ADVANCED SEARCH

If you offer a more advanced search option, provide a link to a separate search page that includes all the advanced options immediately near the search box.

❏ NOT CASE SENSITIVE

Be sure that search results are not case sensitive. This can badly influence the results and prevent visitors from finding what they want by simply making a capitalization error. All searches should perform the same regardless of capitalization used.

❏ FORGIVING OF MISSPELLINGS

Searchers often misspell words, or are simply unsure how product or brand names should be spelled. Your search results should be very forgiving of these errors so the visitor will still find the relevant results they want.

❏ REITERATE SEARCH QUERY

The results page should reiterate the exact search query, bigger and bolder than the results. This allows the visitors to see exactly what they searched and give them a chance to edit their search without retyping the whole thing in the search box.

❏ PROVIDE ALTERNATE SPELLING OPTIONS

After a search is performed, provide options for corrected or alternate spellings that the searcher can click on to refine their results. This can be important for uncommonly spelled brand or product names, or even typical spelling errors.

❏ PROVIDE SEARCH REFINEMENT OPTIONS

Whether the search produces a few or many results, it's a good idea to provide a list of refinement options the searcher can click on to immediately perform the next search. This allows them to narrow down or expand their search without having to think of a new query string themselves. You're providing it for them, while keeping them engaged with your site.

❏ LINK TO RELEVANT PAGES

Search results pages should provide a consistent set of links to other helpful pages of your site. Links to Help and FAQ pages can help them explore your site for more information that may not have been found in the results of their search. Of course, specific information from these pages should also appear in the search results if they are relevant to the query.

❏ NO HTML TABLES

Your search results pages should load fast. Avoid bloating your code using HTML tables. Keep these pages as light and streamlined as possible.

❏ NO BLANK RESULTS

Never produce a page with absolutely no results. If nothing matches the query, state as such, but provide links to other pages, close or related matches or even popular areas of the site. Always give them somewhere to go from here.

❏ EXACT MATCHES DISPLAY FIRST

Results that are an exact match for the query should always be displayed at the very top. These results are likely most relevant to what the visitor is looking for, so don't bury those under other related results, regardless of how popular those pages might be.

❏ SEGMENT "RELATED" RESULTS

Provide a list of results related to the query, though not necessarily a close match, that the visitor might be interested in. This is a good place to show popular content that partially matches the query. Segment this list so the visitor understands the context of these results and how they differ from the rest.

❏ SHOW SIMILAR PRODUCTS

If a search was performed for a specific product, whether your site has an exact match result for that product or not, provide a list of similar products. These results can be displayed as part of the exact match results, or as a sub-set of related products. This is a good way to get additional products in front of your visitor.

❏ SHOW PAGE TITLES AND DESCRIPTIONS

Each result should include the title of the page being linked to, along with that page's meta description (or a snippet of text related to the query.) This is the best way for the visitor to scan the results to find what is most relevant for them. It's worked great for Google; I think it can work for you too!

❏ HIGHLIGHT QUERY IN RESULTS

Bold or highlight the search query words as they appear in any of the results on the page. This helps draw the visitor's eye to the terms they inputted and determine which result is the closest match to their intent.

❏ 10-20 RESULTS PER PAGE

Your search results pages should display 10-20 results total by default. You don't want to overwhelm the searcher, but sometimes 10 results aren't enough. You also want to leave room for additional "flavor" and related content.

❏ CHANGE NUMBER OF RESULTS OPTION

Give the visitor control over the results by allowing them to increase or decrease the number of results displayed per page. Let them increase in multiples of 10 up to 50, then jump to 100 at a time for maximum scanning.

CONTENT WRITING

…Before you begin the writing, be sure you know the purpose or mission or objective of every piece of content that you write. What are you trying to achieve? What information, exactly, are you trying to communicate? And why should your audience care.[9]

–Ann Handley
Everybody Writes

What This Checklist Is About

This checklist covers the writing and creation of content for your website and how to make sure your message is effective at providing the visitor what they want, while fulfilling your business's goals. The points in this checklist are not as easy to verify or quantify as most of the others. Many are subjective, requiring more than just a quick visual confirmation. Take your time going through this list and ask multiple people their thoughts on each point. Ultimately, it doesn't matter what you think, it matters what your audience thinks!

Why Content Is Important

Your website's content is an essential part of your business's persuasion process. The content on the site should interest the reader, draw them in and help them navigate through the conversion process. Without content, you're left with a site that has to sell through images alone. Images are valuable, but they cannot provide everything the visitor needs.

Through your site content, you can appeal to both the emotional and logical centers of the brain, making the case for your business, and your products or services. Content informs, clarifies and, most importantly, sells.

Yet there is more to content than just adding descriptive words to a page. The content has to meet the needs of the audience, and those needs are vast. Some visitors read, some scan, some investigate and others skip it completely. Some visitors require technical data, others require emotional appeals, others require benefits and still others need factual proof. Your content must be crafted for each type of visitor and deliver a seamless experience for all.

Ultimately, your content is usually your first, and sometimes last, point of contact you have with a visitor. It must be as helpful as any salesperson. Good content is the salesperson visitors don't even know they want, and does a job that no salesperson can do: Sell without leaving your visitors feeling sold.

CONTENT WRITING CHECKLIST

❏ BUYER PERSONAS

Before you do any writing, develop a handful of personas that represent your target audience and craft content specifically for them. Consider demographics such as age and education level, as well as specific challenges your product or service can help them overcome. If you develop your personas correctly, you'll be able to match your content to the vast majority of your visitors and adjust your text to match the wants, needs and expectations of those that are most likely to do business with you.

❏ GRAB THE VISITOR'S ATTENTION

The content on each page of your website must immediately grab the visitor's attention. This can be done with a compelling, keyword-friendly headline and a strong opening sentence. Without these, the visitor may quickly wander. Use these two areas — along with striking visuals — to get the reader engaged and give them a reason to keep reading and exploring your site.

Examples
No: *Childrens Bed Frames*
Yes: *Handcrafted Bed Frames for Children of All Ages*
Yes: *Fun and Exciting Childrens Bed Frames*

❏ GET TO THE GOOD STUFF QUICKLY

Don't save the best for last! We live in an instant gratification society; if your best content is saved for the end your readers may never reach the payoff. Start strong and stay strong throughout. Each sentence needs to be compelling enough to lead your visitor to the next one and so on.

❏ OUTLINE IMPORTANCE

Explain to your visitors why the solutions you are offering are important to their way of life. Give them the big picture, setting the stage for your product to provide the answer.

Examples
Your family is important to you, and your health is important to them.
Emergencies don't wait for the most opportune time to occur.
Every year, thousands of businesses get sued.

❏ EXPOSE THE VISITOR'S NEED

Many visitors come to your website because you have something they want. You have to turn that want into a need. It must become a necessity they cannot live without.

What is it about your product or service that your visitor must have? Why is it critical they choose your company over all others that sell the same thing? Your content must (subtly) answer these two questions. A want is optional. A need is not.

Examples
Eliminates discomfort so you get the sleep you need.
Powerful tool batteries that won't quit mid-job.
Coverage that protects your business and your family.

❏ STATE FEATURES CLEARLY

Every product or service has specific features that the reader may want, need or be interested in. Write out the features of each of your offerings to ensure your visitors know and understand all the great benefits of your product or service. Don't hide these features or make visitors hunt for them; they are an important part of the conversion process.

Examples
60" screen in 1080p HD
Light, portable and stores easily
Water resistant

❏ BENEFIT FOCUSED

A fulfilled need can often produce rewards greater than the fulfillment of the need itself. I have a powerful need to eat, but the benefit of tasty food is greater than simply not being hungry. What are the benefits of the products or services you offer? Each product feature should have an inherit benefit. List them out for your audience in specific detail. If you can make their want for what you offer greater than their need for it, you have an offer they can't refuse.

Examples
Easy-to-follow recipes that will have your family asking for more.
Watch any movie, anytime, anywhere.
The perfect haircut every time, or your money back.

❏ ANSWER WIIFM

Visitors will always want to know, "What's in it for me?" You must answer that question in detail. Stay focused on the customer. Keep talk about yourself to a minimum (with the exception of your About Us page), and talk about what the visitor gets from your products or services. Everything should be about them. Don't focus on what you do, but instead focus what they get when they do business with you.

Examples
A theater-quality experience without leaving your home.
Walk in with style and watch heads turn!
Our videos will make you the smartest person in the room.

❏ JUSTIFY THE CONVERSION

Every visitor ultimately must be able to justify their decision to buy your product or service, or otherwise do business with you. Make it an easy decision by incorporating justifications they can use into your content. A visitor who cannot justify pulling the trigger right now won't, regardless of how pressing their need is. Give them the push they need toward that purchase decision.

Examples

You've worked hard, you deserve a little R&R.
Opportunities like these don't happen very often.
Your good health matters!

❏ PROVIDE REASSURANCES

Once justified, provide the visitor with reassurances that you can be trusted and that what you offer is exactly the right solution for them. Take away all their stress, guesswork and hesitation with assurances that they are making the right decision.

Examples

Your wife will appreciate the added comfort she'll receive.
With a 10-year warranty, you know it's money well spent.
You'll never have to worry about infection again.

❏ CALLS TO ACTION

In order for your visitors to take action on your offer, you must give them an action to take. Use active words and be specific as to what the visitor must do next. The goal is to get them to complete the process they have started, and, ultimately, to receive the solution they came looking for. Don't force your visitor to guess where to go or what to do next. Spell it out for them and provide the link(s) to do it.

Examples

Contact us to set up your appointment today.
Download our case study to see our results for yourself.
Learn more about our team and how we can help you today.

❏ APPROPRIATE READING LEVEL

Most people don't realize that not everyone reads at the same level they do. Super-smart people tend to use super-smart words. If that's your audience, great — write super-smartly. But if not, you have to write at the most appropriate reading level for your audience. In most cases, simpler is better because everyone can understand. The more complex your language, the more readers you'll disenfranchise.

❏ DON'T TALK DOWN TO YOUR AUDIENCE

The opposite danger of writing at too high of a reading level is talking down to your audience. Assume you know more than they do (because you likely do), but don't allow any hint of superiority or piety in your words. Speak naturally and helpfully so the visitor feels you're right there with them, not lecturing from above.

Examples

No: *You most certainly never have a chance of understanding the science behind our product. After all, we're the experts.*

Yes: *Understanding all the science behind this product isn't easy, but we're here to help you make sense of it all.*

❏ SHORT SENTENCES

Long sentences are difficult to digest. Use short sentences whenever possible. Break up long strings of thought into multiple thoughts so the reader can more easily understand the concepts written.

Examples

No: *Long sentences can be difficult to digest so use shorter sentences, when possible, to break up long strings of thought into multiple thoughts so the reader can more easily understand the concepts written.*

Yes: *Long sentences can be difficult to digest. Use shorter sentences, when possible, to break up long strings of thought into multiple thoughts. This allows the reader to more easily understand the concepts written.*

❏ CONSISTENT VOICE

While not every page of your site must be written by the same person, the "voice" you use must be consistent throughout. (Blog posts by different authors are the exception.) You must maintain a consistency of content style from page to page in order to provide a seamless reading experience. Content that changes voice can be jarring, if not confusing, to the visitor.

Examples

Technical, humorous, all-business, flowery, personal, etc.

❏ INTEGRATE TOPICALLY RELATED PHRASES (KEYWORDS)

People search using "keywords" that are relevant to the information they are seeking. These search words are valuable, allowing you to craft your content using the same language the visitor uses. Integrate these keywords and any other topically relevant phrases throughout your content to reinforce your message in the visitor's language.

Example
No: *Our dog food is food that your dog will love.*
Yes: *Our dog food is healthy, nutritious and gives your dog more energy.*

❏ ELIMINATE SUPERFLUOUS TEXT

Eliminate any unnecessary words or sentences that over-sell what you are trying to accomplish. Exaggerated statements about your business that cannot be verified by a third party (via a link) lose all impact, and ultimately cause you to lose credibility. Be real with your visitors. You can be great at what you do, but without absolute proof, you're definitely not the best—unless it's your customers saying so.

Example
No: *We make the best steak in Canton, Ohio.*
Yes: *Voted best steakhouse in Canton, Ohio.*

❏ REDUCE/EXPLAIN INDUSTRY JARGON

Avoid the use of industry jargon that the average person does not understand. Your content must be readable to all visitors, even those who are only marginally familiar with your industry. Using unexplained industry jargon doesn't allow your visitor to engage with your offerings and ultimately will push them off to another site that does a better job of speaking on their level.

❏ LINK TO AUTHORITATIVE SOURCES

Authoritative sources often link out to other authoritative sources as a means of bolstering their own authority. You can do the same with your web content. Whenever possible, link out to other sources that reinforce the message you are trying to make. This gives you added credibility as an authority of your own.

Examples

No: *Some random guy I found on the internet said that you should <u>link to authoritative sources to improve your credibility</u>.*

Yes: *Someone that you likely know, from a well-respected company, wrote a white paper on how <u>Linking to Authoritative Sources Improves Your Credibility</u>.*

❏ LINK TO INTERNAL RELATED CONTENT

Whenever referencing content on another page of your site, link to it. No sense making your visitor hunt for whatever it is you're talking about when you can send them directly to it at their convenience. These links can increase interaction and help ensure the visitor gets all the information they need to do business with you.

Examples

No: *On-page optimization without social media marketing is becoming less and less effective.*

Yes: *On-page optimization without <u>social media marketing</u> is becoming less and less effective.*

❏ DISPLAY PUBLICATION DATE ON ARTICLES/NEWS STORIES

People always want to know how relevant any information they are reading is to them today. If you're in an industry that changes fast (technology, fashion, travel, etc.), publication dates can let the visitor know if what they are reading is current or not. Keep in mind, depending on the specific article, an old publication may still be relevant today. Let the reader decide rather than forcing them to read an entire article before realizing that it is no longer relevant.

❏ FIX TYPO, SPELLING AND GRAMMAR ERRORS

Comb through your content to fix all typo, spelling, and grammatical errors. This ensures that your content reads authoritatively. Bad spelling and grammar can quickly leave a bad taste in the reader's mouth. While you may never get your content 100% perfect, strive for that goal.

❏ REVIEW PERIODICALLY

Content can become outdated when changes in your industry and/or business occur. Review your content periodically and update as needed to keep current. Blog content is the exception, as that is expected to go out of date. However, look for opportunities to bring critical posts up to date as well.

CONTENT APPEARANCE

Your audience has little time to waste. They are not reading anything from beginning to end. If they can't find what they want immediately, they are out of there.[10]

–Mary E.S. Morris, Randy J. Hinrichs
Web Page Design

What This Checklist Is About

This list covers aspects of how the content should appear on your website. While the words themselves matter for the enticement and conversion process, how those words are displayed can determine if they are read or ignored, which, in turn, determines whether or not they will have an impact on the conversion process.

Why Content Appearance Is Important

Great content does you and your visitors no good if it isn't easy for the reader to... well, read. Hidden content, content that gets lost in the page, or content that is laid out in an unfriendly manner, can create all sorts of conversion roadblocks for the visitor. Getting your visitors to read your content is critical to your sales process. Or at least it should be. Otherwise, why have content on your site at all?

Ensuring your content fits onto the page visually is just as important as having content that does the job of steering the visitor through the site's conversion funnel. Going through the content writing checklist in the previous chapter will help you make your content search and sales friendly. The appearance of your content must now be formatted to help you achieve your conversion goals.

You must be sure your content is not obstructed by non-essential elements and is formatted in a way that your visitors are able to consume it easily. If the visitor cannot, or has a hard time, reading the content, then it can't do the job it was intended to do. Creating easy-to-read, digestible content will bolster your sales process, which is why you're reading this checklist to begin with.

CONTENT APPEARANCE CHECKLIST

❏ SHORT PARAGRAPHS

Gone are the days of single paragraphs running on forever. Today, we know people digest things better in small chunks. Using short paragraphs helps. There is no "correct" paragraph length, but you generally do not want any paragraph to be longer than 3-5 lines, as displayed on the screen. Keeping paragraphs short enhances readability and keeps the visitor more engaged with your content.

❏ READABLE TEXT SIZE

Your text must be of a sufficient size that all readers with typical or even somewhat impaired vision don't struggle when reading your page. Larger fonts are easier for everyone to read, not just those with poor eyesight. Small fonts, however, can cause you to alienate at least a portion of your audience.

❏ GOOD CONTRAST WITH BACKGROUND

Pay attention to the background behind your text. If using colors or images, you must make sure your text contrasts well and can be seen without any strain. The best contrast is black text on a white background; however, for design purposes this may not be an option. Use contrasting text colors and sizes to maintain the readability of every area of your web page.

❏ SKIMMABLE AND SCANNABLE

Keep your content skimmable and scannable to the eye. Many visitors don't want to read every word to find what they came for, so they look for visual cues that will direct them to that information. Skimmable and scannable content helps these visitors quickly find the needed content and stay engaged with your website.

❏ USE HEADINGS AND SUB-HEADINGS

Headings are important when content on one page is more than a few paragraphs long. It breaks up the monotony and helps the visitor stay engaged with what they're reading. Headings give readers scanning points and topical relevance indicators they can use to jump to areas of greatest interest to them. Use multiple headings to break up long pieces of copy while enhancing its visual appeal.

Examples

This is a Heading 1

This is a Heading 2

This is a Heading 3

❏ LARGE HEADING SIZE

Headings and sub-headings should almost universally be larger than the standard text size. A large heading size shows a heading's visual importance over the text and ensures it stands out from the rest of the page content.

❏ USE BULLETED LISTS

When possible, create bulleted lists of content rather than writing out comma-separated items in paragraph format. A paragraph can easily be skimmed over. Lists help punctuate certain items of text and catch the visitor's eye.

Examples

Good: *Every Christmas morning we read the story of Jesus, pray together, and open gifts.*

Better: *Every Christmas morning we:*
- *Read the story of Jesus*
- *Pray together*
- *Open gifts*

❑ CLOSE LINK PROXIMITY

When using images or buttons to link to other sites, pages, or content, be sure it is in very close proximity to its textual reference. Even better, link the text reference itself to the page you're talking about. You want to make sure the visitor fully understands what each link is for and its relevance to the content. Links that are not in close proximity to the referencing content lose this advantage.

❑ CALLS TO ACTION

Every page should have at least one call to action. What should the visitor do once they are done reading the content? Should they move to another page? Should they scroll down to view a new set of information? Should they add a product to their cart or download a white paper?

Calls to action can be simple hyperlinked references or specific action steps the visitor must take. Tell your visitors what to do and provide the link (if necessary) to do it. Without any call to action, your visitors may genuinely not know what they should do next. Consider adding a button to make your call to action more prominent and enticing to click.

Example
Download the guide now for more information.

LINKS & BUTTONS

Design the links on your pages as though the reader were only reading the links. Identify patterns in your links and make sure you're telling a story with the links.[11]

–Mary E.S. Morris and Randy J. Hinrichs
Web Page Design

WHAT THIS CHECKLIST IS ABOUT

This list covers how links, buttons, and calls to action should be integrated into your site content and design. It includes how to use textual links properly, using calls to action in both image and textual format and how to use these components to your best marketing advantage.

WHY LINKS AND BUTTONS ARE IMPORTANT

Textual links, buttons, and calls to action are an effective way to help your visitors navigate through your site. It enables them to move from page to page, clicking through to content that interests them, while also propelling them through any conversion processes you have created.

Rather than forcing your visitors to disengage from the content and go back to your navigation to hunt for what they want, it is better to keep the visitor continuously engaged by providing further browsing/action options in your content. I call it the Wikipedia effect. It's easy to go to Wikipedia for a quick hit of information and find yourself still reading two hours later, having followed relevant links to multiple pages of interest. Links built into your content give your visitors seamless navigational options, keeping them engaged throughout.

A strong navigation plays an important role in helping your visitors find content they know they want. However, links and action buttons within the content are important for keeping the visitor actively engaged with said content. Such links drive them to content most relevant to their needs, wants and immediate desires.

Links, buttons and calls to action also serve to inform the visitor what actions they should take next in order to achieve their goals. While most people know they can "buy now," having a call to action pushes them to take that action. Calls to action and links keep the engagement momentum moving forward. Anytime the visitor has to guess what they should do next, you lose.

LINKS & BUTTONS CHECKLIST

❏ LINK IMPORTANT COMMANDS

If you are describing something the visitor should do, or an action you want them to take, link the action as it's described. Don't expect the visitor to hunt around for the way to "download" your ebook, or "buy your product" if you don't provide an obvious link to do it.

> **Examples**
> No: *Click the above link to download your free ebook.*
> Yes: *Click here to <u>download your free ebook</u>.*

❏ USE BOTH IMAGES AND LINKS

When creating your calls to action, use both text links, and visual images and buttons. Text links can be beneficial to provide the visitor with an action without disrupting them from the content. Images and buttons can be used more as attention-getters once the visitor has already disengaged and is looking for the next thing to do. Both of these calls are important for interacting with different visitor types.

❏ MAKE THE LINK OBVIOUS

Regardless of whether you're using text or an image to create the link or call to action, be obvious about it. Don't go small. Make sure your action items stand out from the rest of the elements on the page.

❏ USE WHITE SPACE EFFECTIVELY

Using white (blank) space around your calls to action helps draw the visitor to the action that you want them to take. When other elements are too close in proximity, the call to action can get lost or overlooked.

❏ LIMITED NUMBER OF LINKS

It's a good idea to keep the overall number of links on any one page to fewer than 100. This includes navigation, calls to action, product links, etc. In your content area, don't add too many link options. Keep the page focused on the information the visitor needs and provide links only to those things that are relevant for them to complete the action you desire.

❏ UNDERLINE LINKS IN TEXT

Underlined content is a universal indicator that text is a link. Non-underlined links in your text tend to blend into the content, and the visitor may not understand it to be a call to action. Even when the link is a different color, the visitor may simply assume you did that for emphasis and not realize it is a link. Underlining your links ensures your visitors know what is an action and what isn't.

Example
No: *Emphasis is not enough* to indicate a link.
Yes: *It's always best to <u>underline links</u>*.

❏ LINK TO RELATED CONTENT

If content on one page references content on another, link to that other page. This gives your visitors an opportunity to easily learn more without having to go back to the navigation and hunt for how to find that information.

Examples

No: *On-page optimization without social media marketing is becoming less and less effective.*

Yes: *On-page optimization without <u>social media marketing</u> is becoming less and less effective.*

❏ LINK TEXT REFLECTS LINKED CONTENT

Use link text that accurately reflects the content of the page you are linking to. Using descriptive text in the link itself helps the visitor understand more about what they are clicking to, even without having to read the text around the link. Let them click on the actual text they will be learning more about.

Example

No: *<u>Click here</u> to view our quality standards page.*

Yes: *You'll be impressed by our <u>high quality standards</u>.*

❏ KEYWORDS IN LINKS

When linking to other pages—whether to internal pages or to an external website—use keywords in the link text. This helps bolster the search engine relevance of the page being linked to, and, again, is a clue to the visitor as to what content they will get if they do click the link. Just be careful not to link only your keywords. It's a good idea to add supportive content into the link as well.

Example

No: *Check out our <u>products</u>.*

Yes: *Check out our <u>snowboard gear</u>.*

❏ SEARCH-FRIENDLY LINK CODE

Be sure the code you use to create your links is search engine friendly (i.e., it can be followed by search engines.) This ensures the search engines can index all your important content pages to include in the search results. Pages that don't have search-friendly link code can be left out of the search index or be valued lower than they otherwise would.

Example

No: `<a href="javascript:void(0)" onclick="myJsFunc();">`

Yes: `<a href="http://www.site.com/page.html">`

❏ BLOCK SEARCH ENGINES FROM CARTS

When using "add to cart," "add to wishlist," or "view cart" links, be sure to use code that prevents these links from being followed by the search engines. The engines have no need to access or index any content in those areas. Preventing them from getting into those areas keeps the search engines focused on indexing and ranking the pages that matter most.

❏ CHECK FOR BROKEN LINKS

Check your site regularly for broken links. The internet is constantly changing with pages being removed and relocated all the time—even on your own site. A monthly broken link check gives you the opportunity to keep your links current, while ensuring you're not driving visitors to pages that no longer exist, whether onsite or off.

❏ USE CONSISTENT LINKING PRACTICES

Use canonical URLs in all links throughout your site. Whichever URL format you choose to make as the canonical version, be sure to use it consistently. While 301 redirects and canonical tags can tell the search engines which URL is to receive the "value," maintaining a consistent link structure is preferable and is less prone to mistakes.

Example

Link this: `<a href="http://site.com/page.html">`

or this: `<a href="http://www.site.com/page.html">`

but not both.

SOCIAL SHARING CONSIDERATIONS

Always controversial, the number of social shares a page accumulates tends to show a positive correlation with rankings. Although there is strong reason to believe Google doesn't use social share counts directly in its algorithm, there are many secondary SEO benefits to be gained through successful social sharing. [12]

> –Moz Search Engine Ranking Factors Report

WHAT THIS CHECKLIST IS ABOUT

This checklist covers how to make your website more shareable and engagement friendly for social media, specifically in relation to adding social signals to your site's content. It covers integration of specific buttons, types of code, and social links that will be valuable to your business as you seek to help your audience evangelize your products and services.

Please note that social networks change frequently. You should check with each platform to know which buttons, tags, etc., are available for you to incorporate into your website.

WHY SOCIAL SHARING IS IMPORTANT

Search engines are increasingly looking to social signals to help determine the value of a website or page for a particular search query. How much weight, or the exact impact these signals have on search results, continues to be a hotly debated topic. But put aside any

The Best Damn Web Marketing Checklist, Period! 2.0

potential search engine ranking benefit that your socially shared content might receive, because it does provide a more immediate benefit: traffic.

It's not enough to create good content (text, video, images, etc.) and wait for the search engines to find it, hope they index it and pray they rank it well. You need to get that content in front of relevant eyeballs sooner rather than later. Social media provides that opportunity.

Sharing your own content on social networks is of decent benefit. Search engines do monitor social channels to see what's being published. But the real benefit of social sharing comes when your audience starts pushing your content to their audiences, thereby increasing your sphere of influence. Your content reaches a broader audience than it ever would otherwise, as your followers become your evangelists.

Without social sharing options, however, that evangelism process isn't quite so easy. Yes, your content can still be shared on your visitor's social profiles, but specific social buttons act as a call to action to your readers, reminding them to share what they like, while also making it very easy for them to do so.

SOCIAL SHARING CHECKLIST

❏ USE SHARE BUTTONS

To make it easier to share the content on your website, add social sharing buttons that allow your visitors to publish your content to their social streams. Focus on the social networks where your target audience is most engaged. For example, if you are a technical company targeting engineers, a LinkedIn share button might get more mileage than one for Pinterest. If you sell women's clothing, the reverse would be true.

Add your sharing buttons only to the pages that makes sense to do so, as not all pages need them. No one really wants to "share" your contact us page, but they may want to share your products and even product category pages. Be sure to use buttons that automatically tag your account (Twitter) when your content is shared.

❏ USE FOLLOW BUTTONS

Make it easy for your visitors to connect with your brand and to follow you (or your business) on each social channel you are active on. If you are relatively inactive on a social network, don't link to it. Stick to those where you are actively engaged! Add buttons linking to your social profiles that can be easily found on every page of your website. Typically, these are best placed in your site's footer.

– PAGE 88 –

❏ IMPLEMENT OPEN GRAPH META DATA

Facebook, LinkedIn, and other social networks use open graph meta data from your site when displaying previews of links in posts. If open graph meta data is not available, the social networks guess at what the correct information to display is and the results are not always favorable. Add open graph tags for title, type, description, image and URL, to have greater control on how links to your websites are displayed on social media.

❏ IMPLEMENT FACEBOOK META DATA

If you have a Facebook page for your business, you will want to include the fb:admins meta data to connect your Facebook page to your web page. This meta data allows you to have access to additional information in Facebook Insights.

❏ IMPLEMENT TWITTER CARD META DATA

Twitter cards allow for expanded detail and media on tweets, like a link preview with content summary on other social networks, product information, or media player to name a few. After implementing the appropriate tags, you'll need to apply for approval with Twitter for the additional information to display in tweets.

❏ IMPLEMENT PINTEREST RICH PIN META DATA

If your target market is active on Pinterest, add rich pin meta tags to your site for apps, products, recipes, movies, articles, and places. Implementing these tags will allow additional information such as recipe ingredients and instructions to be included in the pin itself on Pinterest. This makes your content more engaging and shareable on the platform.

HOME PAGE

> Today's online shopper spends approximately 25 seconds perusing a new ecommerce website before deciding to either make a purchase or move on to another store. And just about every one of those seconds is spent scrutinizing the home page.[13]
>
> 3dcart

What This Checklist Is About

This list covers a few quick points, each specifically relevant to your website's home page. These points tell you how to create a home page that presents your offerings and is able to push visitors to the information they need, quickly.

Why Your Home Page Is Important

Your site's home page is one of the single most visited pages of your site (not counting blog posts) and, in many cases, the first page a visitor will see. For many sites, the home page can get the highest number of entrances over any other page.

Whether a visitor lands on your home page first or navigates to it from an internal page, they are there expecting to get a global view of what you offer. Many searchers will land on an internal page most relevant to their needs but move to the home page to get a sense of who you are and what you are all about.

Your home page should give the "big picture" view of your company and what you do. It should also act as the doorway to more information about you, your products or services, and how you are able to meet the visitor's needs. It should act as something of a sneak-peak at what the visitors will see once they click further into the site.

Organize your home page wisely. Don't try to present everything; instead, use it as a portal that helps the visitor quickly get to the information that is most relevant to their needs.

HOME PAGE CHECKLIST

❏ INSTANT PAGE IDENTIFICATION

Your visitors should immediately be able to tell when they land on your home page. This should be made obvious by the content, headers and the layout of the page. Home pages generally stand out from the rest of the site while maintaining cohesion with it at the same time. That difference should be enough to uniquely identify your home page from the rest.

❏ SITE OVERVIEW

Your home page is the all-encompassing portal to the other pages of your site. It should not be used as a sitemap to every page, nor should you try to explain everything about your business or what you do—use internal pages for that. Instead, use the home page to provide highlights that entice the visitor to click further into the site to gain specific information and knowledge. Provide enough information to show credibility to your visitors and make them want to go further to learn more.

❏ KEEP CONTENT CONSISTENT

There is no need to keep changing the content of your home page to get the attention of the search engines. If you pull in blog post titles or recent tweets, that's fine, but don't change your home page content for the sake of change. Keep a strong, consistent message. You're free to test new ideas for conversion, but otherwise, develop a message and stick with it.

❏ NO SPLASH PAGE

A splash page is an "introductory" page that generally uses flash or other graphical elements as a visitor "welcome" screen. These pages usually link only to the home page, causing an additional click for your visitors before they can even see what you offer. It also creates an unneeded funnel into your site, hindering both search engines and visitors alike.

Remove all splash pages and let your visitors land directly onto your home page. While splash pages are generally a thing of the past, we all know that even bad trends often return. Don't let it be this one!

❏ ADD SOCIAL BUTTONS

If you don't use social buttons on any other page (and you should!), you absolutely need to include them on your home page. These social buttons allow your visitors to follow you on the social channels of your choice and engage with you off-site at their leisure.

ABOUT US PAGE

While the usability of "About Us" pages has improved 9% over the past five years, paradoxically, user satisfaction has actually dropped from 5.2 to 4.6 (on a 1-7 scale).[14]

–Jeremy Johnson
Rocketspark

WHAT THIS CHECKLIST IS ABOUT

This checklist covers several elements specific to your website's about us page. It provides information regarding content, placement, and usability that are necessary to deliver what visitors expect to find when they visit this page. These check points will help you create a better about us page that will help your visitors assess your company's ability to meet their needs and instill confidence in doing business with you.

WHY YOUR ABOUT US PAGE IS IMPORTANT

Studies have proven that visitors who have visited a site's about us page are more likely to convert than those that don't. This can signify that those who visit your about us page are already more engaged and looking for that final piece of confidence to pull the trigger. But it can also be a strong indicator that your about us page can have a significant impact on influencing your visitors toward the final conversion, whatever that is for you.

Your about us page should help visitors "get to know" you and your company—provided, of course, you have the right information in place. The entire conversion process is about giving potential customers the assurances they need to go ahead and purchase your product or service. Your about us page must provide many of those assurances.

Because this page is designed to help your visitors learn more about you, your about us page should provide the information that achieves this goal. Sparsely populated about us pages don't really give the visitor what they want and are therefore more apt to cause the visitor to leave feeling less, rather than more, inclined to do business with you.

The more information you provide on your about us page, broken into skimmable and scannable chunks, the better informed your visitors will be, having learned what kind of company you are and what you can do for them. The better the feelings that your about us page is able to elicit from the visitor, the more likely you are to gain them as a customer.

ABOUT US PAGE CHECKLIST

❏ FULL COMPANY DESCRIPTION

Be robust in the information you provide about your company. Tell the story of how you came to be, highlighting the struggles, milestones and successes you've had along the way. The more details you provide, the more engaged each visitor will be as they read. Instead of feeling as if they're doing business with a corporation, they'll see you as invested in providing quality products and services.

❏ TEAM BIOGRAPHIES

You may not be able to include biographies for every member of your team, but you should definitely include the biographies of those in leadership positions. This puts real faces to your company story and lets people "meet" those who are in charge of making sure customers are happy. It also lets your customers know that you won't hide behind the anonymity of the internet, but will hold your team accountable in making sure every customer is a satisfied customer.

❏ MISSION STATEMENT

Your business needs a purpose for existing beyond that of making profits. Let your visitors know what that purpose is so they can see if your values align with their own. Talk about what makes you different from your competition and why they should choose to do business with you. Mission statements let your visitors know what you believe in, giving them more reasons to do business with you.

❏ Up-To-Date Information

Be sure to keep your about us page current and up to date. Don't use language such as, "We started 15 years ago," but rather, "We started in 1995." The latter stays current no matter what year it is today. Also, be sure to remove outdated references such as "We just moved into our new facility." Again, specific dates are better than time references.

❏ Link to Supporting Pages

Don't try to get all your important company information on a single about us page. Some information deserves a page (or pages) of its (their) own. Use your about us page to link to other important areas of content that the visitor might want to know about.

❏ Contact Us Page

While you should already have a prominent link to your contact us page in your main navigation, linking to that page from your about us page can keep your visitors engaged and move them to the next stage of conversion.

❏ Registration Info

If you have a member's only section of your site, or require visitors to login/register before they can complete a purchase, provide a link to your registration page. This page should include more than a registration form, but should also extol the virtues of creating an account with you.

❏ Investor Relations

If your company has investors or is a publicly traded company, provide a link to a page that includes information that is beneficial to your stockholders and investors.

❏ Company News

Whether you have a specific section on your site dedicated to company news, or you publish news posts on your blog, provide a link so visitors can easily learn more about the things that make your company newsworthy.

❏ JOB OPPORTUNITIES

Link to your job opportunities page so would-be applicants have a way to contact you specifically for work opportunities. This page should cover how to apply for a job, where to send a resume, and other information needed for entry-level and management positions.

❏ NEWSLETTERS

If you offer a newsletter (outside of blog updates), provide a link to a page that allows your visitors to sign up to receive them. You also might want to make past newsletters available here.

❏ PRICING

Many visitors like to see a pricing overview when looking at serviced-based websites. This can include hourly rates for different services, or pricing for specific type of work. Even if it's just "starts at," including a link to a pricing page can help visitors assess whether they can do business with you or not more quickly and save you the hassle of dealing with a bad lead.

❏ TESTIMONIALS

It's probably a good idea to have a link to your testimonials page available in your main navigation, but you should also link to it from your about us page. The website is a journey. Your job is to move visitors along to the pages that will help them become customers. Visitors on your about us page are likely also interested in looking at testimonials as well.

❏ LINK TO SOCIAL NETWORKS

Give your visitors an opportunity to follow your company on the social networks you are active on. This is a great way to move your visitors from single engagement to active engagement via your social channels.

❏ NOTE ASSOCIATIONS, CERTIFICATIONS & AWARDS

Has your company (or any team member) accomplished anything noteworthy, received any certifications, or become part of any relevant groups or associations? If so, this information should be highlighted on your about us page to lend additional credibility to your company. Whenever possible, link to the certification, association or award source to allow for independent verification.

CONTACT US PAGE

If you want to increase form conversions, you must consider reducing the number of fields.[15]

–Oli Gardner
Unbounce

What This Checklist Is About

This list covers important aspects of what visitors expect and need to encounter when visiting your contact us page. The goal is to increase the effectiveness of this page by helping visitors contact you through whatever method is most convenient for them, while also providing additional signals of trust and security about your company.

Why Your Contact Us Page Is Important

Visitors who land on your contact us page are showing clear intent in wanting to get in touch with you at some point in the future, if not right away. Some visitors are simply seeking immediate knowledge as to what level of access you're offering them, should the need arise. Lacking available—but important—contact options, these potential customers might turn away believing that your company isn't as accessible as you believe yourself to be.

Not everyone who lands on your contact us page will actually follow through in doing so. However, the easier you make it for a visitor to open up one-to-one engagement with your company, the more likely you are to earn them as a customer. Your contact us page doesn't have to be loaded with content, but it does need to be loaded with contact options and other relevant information.

Use your contact us page to solicit active engagement. As annoying as it may be to field calls or emails with questions that are readily answered on your website, you can be sure that demonstrating your availability to visitors can significantly improve your visitor-to-customer conversion ratio.

CONTACT US PAGE CHECKLIST

❏ EASY TO FIND

Links to your contact us page should be relatively easy to find. Don't hide them in drop-down menus that can't be seen without actively clicking around your navigation. The easier it is for visitors to contact you, the more chances you have to convert them into customers.

❏ MULTIPLE CONTACT OPTIONS

Don't limit your visitor's ability to contact you to your preference only. Each customer has a preferred way of contacting companies depending on their situation. Some may be "urgent," requiring a phone call, while others may be able to wait for a slower response via email. Giving your visitors multiple contact options makes them feel confident that they can reach you in whatever way they need.

❏ TELEPHONE NUMBER(S)

Provide your visitors both local and toll-free phone numbers on your contact us page. If you only do business locally, a local phone number is sufficient. If you have multiple offices, it's a good idea to include the main number for each location.

Example
Toll Free: 800-555-1212
Seattle Office: 206-555-1212
Cleveland Office: 216-555-1212

❏ FAX NUMBER

While the first point of contact is rarely initiated by fax, there may be a time when someone does need to fax you a document. If you don't include your fax number on your contact us page, you'll have to field the phone call needed just to ask for information that should have been readily available on the site.

❏ **EMAIL ADDRESS**

Showing your actual company email address on your contact us page (rather than providing a contact form only) allows visitors to add your full contact information into their address book for future use. The email address itself should be hyperlinked so the visitor's email client (Outlook, Gmail, etc.) will automatically open when clicked, with the address filled in. Worried about spam? Get a good filter. Your customers are more important!

> **Example**
> No: *info [at] pole position marketing [dot] com*
> Yes: *info@polepositionmarketing.com*

❏ **WEB FORMS**

Provide a contact form that allows visitors to send a message to your team directly from your contact us page. This is a great way to collect visitor data into your database for future follow-up or promotions. Most visitors are content using forms, but the web form should never be your only contact option.

❏ **INSTANT CHAT**

Instant chat gives your customers real-time access to any member of your team. It can also reduce the number of calls or emails your company receives by giving your visitors instant answers while they are actively interacting with your site. In most cases, online chat also allows one person to help multiple people at once, where a phone call helps only one person at a time.

❏ **SOCIAL MEDIA PROFILES**

More and more, people are using social media as a way to communicate and engage directly with the brands they love. Adding links to your social profiles encourages your customers to connect with you socially as well.

❏ **MULTIPLE POINTS OF CONTACT**

If your company has multiple departments that each have their own numbers or extensions, provide the direct number/extension for each one. This allows your visitors to get to the right place without forcing them to navigate through an annoying phone tree, or being placed in on-hold hell.

Here is a list of the type of contact points you can offer:

- ❏ **CUSTOMER SERVICE**
- ❏ **TECH SUPPORT**
- ❏ **INQUIRIES**
- ❏ **MANAGEMENT TEAM MEMBERS**

- ❏ **GENERAL INFORMATION**
- ❏ **JOB APPLICATIONS**
- ❏ **BILLING**
- ❏ **HUMAN RESOURCES**

❏ HOURS OF OPERATION

If your business hours are limited or you only answer the phone during specific times, specify this information on your contact us page. You also might want to let visitors know how soon they can expect a response.

Examples
Business Hours: M-F 9am-5pm
Support Hours: M-Th 10am-4pm

❏ STREET MAP

If your business supports local customers, provide a map to your physical location. This helps local visitors find your location more easily, and can also help your site in local search results.

❏ FINAL CALL TO ACTION

Encourage your visitors to contact you *today*, via any of the avenues mentioned above. This lets them know you are accessible and won't try to dodge actual customer interaction, as many other companies do.

❏ REQUIRE ONLY ESSENTIAL INFO

Don't burden your visitors by trying to collect unneeded information. This is especially true of web forms. Ask only for information that is essential for the best person to reach them. All other questions can wait.

ECOMMERCE CONSIDERATIONS

61% of customers read online reviews before making a purchase decision... while 63% of customers are more likely to make a purchase from a site which has user reviews.[16]

–Graham Charlton
Econsultancy

What This Checklist Is About

This checklist is specifically for ecommerce websites to help make sure you have the most basic elements of ecommerce covered. The items in this list are designed to give you a starting point for improving your ecommerce and online sales processes. They will help your visitors stay engaged in the conversion process on your site, and avoid snags that would inhibit the visitor from completing the purchase they came to make.

Why Ecommerce Is Important

If you sell products on your website, the ecommerce platform you use plays a vital role in helping or harming your site's conversion metrics. Selling a product requires more than simply putting product information and details on your site with a "buy" option next to the product photo. You have to make the total buying process simple and easy.

If you can land visitors on your site but are unable to convince them to add products to the cart, click the "checkout" button, provide you with all the required information, or click that final "submit order" button, then all the money spent getting those visitors to your site is of little value.

Your ecommerce platform must be effectively utilized—or improved—so you can provide visitors with the necessary information, persuade them they need what you're selling, and keep them committed to the purchase throughout the checkout process. And every step of the sales process must be (re)evaluated, (re)tweaked and (continuously) improved.

Each change you make must be tested to make sure it increases your conversion rates from the version prior. Improving the overall ecommerce experience on your site will, by default, improve your sales figures, as you allow for fewer hindrances and hesitations in purchasing your products.

ECOMMERCE CONSIDERATIONS CHECKLIST

❏ MINICART DISPLAY

When a product is added to the shoppers "cart," be sure this action is made clear without pushing the visitor to another page. This can be done with a sidebar that displays all items in the cart or a simple pop-up message that notifies them that the product was added. The goal is to make sure the "add to cart" action does not disengage the visitor from the product page they are viewing.

❏ DISPLAY PAYMENT OPTIONS

Be clear as to which payment options you accept. A good way to do this is to display visual payment option logos in a global navigation area so it shows on every page, including the shopping cart. This provides comfort to the visitors, before they even begin shopping, that you accept the payment method of their choice.

❏ MAJOR CREDIT CARDS

Display the logos of the credit cards you accept. Many shoppers use specific cards for payment. If you don't accept AmEx or Discover, they need to know. If you do, they will want to know that as well so they can continue shopping, confident they will have a hassle-free checkout.

❏ THIRD-PARTY PAYMENT PROCESSORS

Many visitors don't like using credit cards online, but they are happy to pay with third-party solutions such as PayPal, Apple Pay or Google Wallet. Supporting these options will allow you to provide alternate payment options for shoppers who are so inclined. If you accept either, be sure you make this clear; if not, it might be a good time to add them to your payment options arsenal.

❏ ELIMINATE DUPLICATE PRODUCT URLS

Many ecommerce systems create multiple URLs for the exact same product, depending on the category or path used to find it on the site. While a canonical tag can tell the search engines which URL is the "correct" one, the best solution is to eliminate this kind of duplication altogether. This ensures that any link value each product might receive is maintained in one URL, not split between two or more.

❏ DON'T USE URL TRACKING IDS

Some ecommerce systems rely on session and tracking IDs in the URL to keep track of products placed in the shopper's cart. These URLs create duplicate content issues that are best avoided. Look for alternate means of tracking shopper interaction on the site, such as cookies.

❏ EXCLUDE CART PAGES FROM SEARCH ENGINES

Search engines should not be allowed to follow links that add products to carts or wishlists, or that view products in the shopping cart. Use coding that keeps the search engines from recognizing or following these links.

❏ EXCLUDE LINKS TO DUPLICATE SECURE URLS

If you are currently only using secure URLs within your shopping cart, be sure to maintain a distinct separation between secure and non-secure URLs. Don't allow the same pages to be accessed by both. Links back to your product pages from inside the secure shopping cart should direct the visitor to the primary product URL, not link to the secure version by default. Better yet, consider switching to full HTTPS for your entire site.

❏ ALLOW USER-GENERATED CONTENT

The best ecommerce sites do more than sell products. They are a way for shoppers to engage with the business and other shoppers as well. User-generated content comes in various forms. You can decide which are right for your site, but I would consider each of them and implement any and all that you can.

❏ REVIEWS

Allow shoppers to write their own reviews of your products/services.

❏ RATINGS

Similar to reviews, you can also have shoppers rate the products.

❏ QUESTIONS

Some shoppers might have questions that they need to have answered before they'll be willing to buy the product. Giving them a space to ask those questions not only increases the likelihood you'll get that sale, it will likely help others with the same questions.

❏ STORIES

Let visitors post their own experiences with your product or service. This is less of a review than it is a way to highlight creative ways your products were used and what problems they solved for others.

❏ PICTURES

Along with stories, you can let your visitors post pictures that illustrate your products in use.

❏ VIDEOS

If you allow videos, some users will use this for any and all of the above. They can post a video review, tell their stories, and show the product in action. If a picture is worth a thousand words, a video has got to be worth so much more!

❏ KEEP SECURITY CERTIFICATE CURRENT

Be sure to keep your site security certificate up to date. Any lapse in this can disrupt the sales process and call your entire site's security into question. Even a temporary issue here can cause you to lose customers for life.

❑ INSTALL ECOMMERCE TRACKING

Where applicable, install ecommerce tracking codes so you can track metrics such as transactions, revenue and average sale value. This data can be extremely important as you determine the value of each visitor. It also provides insight on how best to funnel your advertising and marketing budgets to reach those that bring the highest profits.

ECOMMERCE PRODUCT CATEGORY PAGES

A category page is more than simply a list of products and features for shoppers to compare, it induces the desire to purchase your products.[17]

—Optimonk

What This Checklist Is About

This checklist covers items related specifically to your ecommerce sites' product category pages. The goal is to help visitors quickly find the products that fit their need or desire and move on to the actual product pages. You want to create pages that provide sufficient value and encourage the shopper to continue their shopping process, rather than getting hung up on any lack of effectiveness of the category page they are on.

Why Category Product Pages Are Important

Every product category page can be a landing page in its own right. Searchers who do not yet know the specific products they want can find a well-crafted category page helpful in narrowing down their search.

A properly constructed category page not only informs the shopper what products are available, but it actually helps them make product purchase decisions. How the product information is displayed and what information is available (as well as what isn't) all influence the shopper's decision on whether to dive deeper into your product offerings or not.

Overall, every product category page on your site should have a very particular focus. The goal is to display products that fit only the narrowness (or broadness) of the category and provide whatever information about the products necessary to entice visitors to click-through to the products themselves. Within that framework, there are some very specific optimization strategies that you need to employ to get each page to serve its purpose more effectively.

ECOMMERCE PRODUCT CATEGORY PAGE CHECKLIST

❏ SIMPLIFIED CATEGORIES

Keep your product categories simple. Don't provide so many category selection options that your visitors become overwhelmed. When a large number of categories are needed, group them into smaller master categories and then use sub-categories to filter the visitor down into the specific products they need.

❏ ON-SCROLL IMAGES

Many ecommerce sites resort to forcing visitors to click through page after page to see more products. Instead, display all products relevant to a particular product category, but keep images from being displayed until those products appear in the viewable area of the screen. This allows for faster loading of pages while also keeping visitors on one page.

❏ ADJUST NUMBER OF PRODUCTS PER PAGE

If you absolutely must resort to having multiple pages of products, at the very least allow your visitors to change the number of products to be viewed on each page. I suggest defaulting high (unless you have slow-loading pages), and let your visitors adjust down as desired.

❏ ALLOW PRODUCT FILTERING

When you have a lot of products, you should implement a way to filter them based on specific criteria. Determine in advance which filters would benefit from being their own optimized landing page and which filters should just affect which products are displayed on the existing page.

❏ PRODUCT SEARCH

If you have a large number of products in a product category, allow shoppers to search within that specific category for features that aren't available with the pre-determined product filters.

❏ PRODUCT COMPARISONS

Allow shoppers to select two to four (or more) products to compare against each other. For best results, the comparison should work like a shopping cart. Allow shoppers to add a product to the comparison "cart" and then switch over to the compare page as desired.

❏ ADJUST SORT ORDER

Give your shoppers the option to change how products are displayed on the page. Having a variety of sort options allows them to more quickly find products that fit a specific criteria. Provide options such as sorting by price, size, new, top selling, rating, etc.

❏ SHOW PRODUCT RATINGS

If you allow shoppers to rate and review your products, show the star rating average with the product on the category page. This can help eliminate excessive clicking and hunting through multiple products, and help visitors zero in on a few they want to compare.

❏ CLOSEOUT PAGES

Build separate pages specifically for products that are on sale or closeout. Many searchers are looking for your products on sale. By creating closeout pages, you can capture this search traffic and drop them on a page that directly meets their need.

PRODUCT PAGES

Nearly ***60% of the buyer's journey is complete before they ever talk to a salesperson.*** That means the product page has to do a lot of the heavy lifting when it comes to satisfying the questions a prospective customer has before they contact your company.[18]

–Meghan Keaney Anderson
HubSpot

WHAT THIS CHECKLIST IS ABOUT

This list covers items that are relevant to product description pages, as opposed to category or sub-category level pages. The items in this list will help you make each product page a more efficient sales page, while also attracting, engaging and convincing the customer to buy the product being offered.

WHY YOUR PRODUCT PAGES ARE IMPORTANT

A product page has a very singular goal: to sell a product. That product might have varying colors, sizes or options, but, for the most part, each product page is dedicated to one product only. In order to sell that product, the page must include many elements placed in just the right way.

Each product page must introduce the product, describe it, relay the features and benefits, and ultimately convince the visitor that this product is the solution they are looking for. It must also play a role in convincing the visitor to buy the product they're looking for from your company rather than from your competition. To get the sale, you must have the right product and be the right company to buy from. That's not easy when there are dozens of other potential "right" companies selling the "right" product as well.

Convincing your visitor to buy from you is accomplished by a number of things—such as layout, images, data placement and other security issues—each playing an important role. In fact, the product page must accomplish many things, yet it must do them all without complicating or cluttering the sales process in any way.

As always, test every change. It's best to test changes on a limited number of products or shoppers. Once you have enough data, you can determine if that change should be rolled out site-wide. The following best practices will give you a good starting point, but then continue to test additional changes to continue to improve your sales.

PRODUCT PAGE CHECKLIST

❏ ONE MASTER CATEGORY

Every product should be assigned to one master category that will be used to determine which category that product is most associated with. You can assign products to multiple categories, allowing them to show up on any category page for which it fits. However, you should have a single master category that will be used to determine the canonical URL of each product.

❏ CONSISTENT PAGE LAYOUT

Be consistent on your product page layouts. Make sure the information you provide is in the same place on every page. When pages are not consistent, it forces the shopper to reorient themselves to find information that would otherwise be easy to locate. Make shopping easy by keeping information consistently in the same place.

❏ SHORT, KEYWORD-FRIENDLY URLs

Don't use an ecommerce system that creates long, cumbersome URLs that a visitor couldn't retype if they tried. Short and keyword-friendly URLs reinforce your product brand names, help search engines understand the context of the page, and increase visitor usability on your site.

Example
No: *www.site.com/bvs294835/*
Yes: *www.site.com/movies/batman-vs-superman*

❏ **DISPLAY CONTACT INFO**

You never know when a potential customer will need to have one last question answered before they commit to purchasing a product. Displaying a phone number your visitors can see can make the difference between getting a sale and losing a customer.

If you're completely unwilling to display your phone number, at least provide an obvious link to your contact us page, where the visitor can find alternate ways to reach you. Be aware that when shoppers are ready to commit, any delay in answering a pertinent question may result in the loss of the sale.

❏ **COMBINE SKUS FOR SIMILAR PRODUCTS**

When products come in various shapes and sizes, each variation comes with its own SKU for tracking purposes. Despite this, incorporate all SKUs for these types of variations into a single product page. Don't have a separate product page for a large size and a small size, or red versus blue. Let the shopper pick those from the one product page and track the SKU internally.

❏ **CLEAR PRODUCT PRESENTATION**

Your product page should be relatively clean and full of whitespace, despite the amount of information that must be shown. Organize your content into clean blocks using design elements to call attention to those areas that are most relevant.

❏ **SHOW PRODUCT RATINGS AND REVIEWS**

If you allow shoppers to rate and review your products, provide this information (or a link to it) with each product. Many shoppers use ratings and reviews to influence their purchase decisions. If this information is not available, it may be cause for them to go elsewhere to purchase the same product.

❏ **ADD VIDEOS**

Videos can help bring traffic to your site and sell your products or services. When applicable, add videos specific to your products that give the visitor information they couldn't get otherwise. You can use videos to demonstrate the product in use, provide your own product reviews, or just demonstrate how the product looks in the real world.

❑ OBVIOUS CALL TO ACTION

Don't hide your "add to cart" or other call to action items. These should be clear and very near the product information that it represents. Calls to action that are too far down the page, or too far removed from the product information itself, are easily overlooked. You don't want the visitor to hunt for this action; make it easy for them to take this action.

❑ MULTIPLE CALLS TO ACTION

If your product page is loaded with great information that the visitor must scroll down to read, it can be helpful to add a second "add to cart" button at the bottom of the page with the relevant options. No sense forcing them back to the top to take action.

❑ CLEAR PRICING

Product pricing should be clearly distinguishable from the rest of the product information. If you have different pricing options on one product, be sure each is clearly displayed. Once an option or quantity is selected, the true price should be updated and displayed bigger and bolder than other prices listed.

❑ DISPLAY INTERNATIONAL PRICING

If you ship internationally, be sure to provide international pricing in the currency of the countries you ship to, or allow the visitor to select the currency of their choice. This allows shoppers to know exactly how much an item costs in figures they understand, without forcing them to do conversion math themselves.

❑ HIGH-DEF PRODUCT IMAGES

Use the highest-quality images possible to showcase your products on the page. This may mean getting an expensive camera and creating an in-house photography studio, but it'll be money well-spent. With so many HD monitors—and even TVs—being used for web browsing, high-quality images are essential to present your products in the best possible way.

❑ MULTIPLE IMAGE VIEWS

If one image speaks a thousand words, then multiple images speak millions. Provide alternate image views such as multiple angles, zoomed in or out, different colors and even an image of the product in use. These images can often give the shopper a clearer idea of what the product will truly look like in "real life."

❑ DESCRIBE THE IMAGE CONTENT

Don't rely on the image to do all the talking. Use a few words of your own to describe the image detail. Even better, describe the *feeling* the product evokes, using words that the image itself cannot convey.

❑ ROBUST PRODUCT DESCRIPTION

Product descriptions are critical to providing the shopper with the information they need to help them decide if the product is right for them. Provide more than a cheap salesy paragraph; instead, be robust in your product descriptions. Also be sure that, even among similar products, the description for each product is unique.

❑ PRODUCT DETAILS AND SPECIFICATIONS

Sometimes a description of the product isn't enough information for the visitor to make an informed decision. Product specifications, visual details, and how to use or install the product can be beneficial to closing the sale. Incorporate as much detail as possible into your product pages to give visitors whatever information they may need. This information also helps cuts down on product returns from uninformed buyers.

❑ PROVIDE ON-DEMAND CONTENT

If you have a lot of product information to display, you'll want to chunk your content into sections that can be accessed on-demand. Typically, you'll see this implemented in a tab structure with specifications, reviews, and benefits each utilizing their own tab. But you can do this for long product descriptions as well. Use descriptive paragraph headings to keep content hidden until the heading is clicked to reveal the relevant content. Just be sure to use a clear notifier so the visitor knows more content is available.

❏ IMPLEMENT CANONICAL TAG

When it is impossible to implement the duplication issue fixes above, you'll need to implement a canonical tag for all products. Again, this should be based on the master product category and single product page, rather than a canonical tag for every variation of each product.

❏ EMPHASIZE BRAND QUALITY AND TRUST

Use the trust behind the brand names you sell to your advantage. Emphasize the known qualities of those brands and, if possible, link to the brands' home pages for things such as warranties, guarantees and product history.

❏ OFFER PRODUCT SELECTION OPTIONS

If one product comes in various flavors (colors, sizes, etc.), be sure those options are readily available. For the shopper's convenience, it is beneficial to make sure these options are available on a single product page rather than creating a separate product page for each color or size.

❏ SHOW SHIPPING COSTS

If you offer fixed- or flat-rate shipping, it's helpful for the visitor to have this information before they begin adding products to their cart. Other shipping options and costs should be clear as well. If shipping is based on location, provide a way for the visitor to enter their zip code to get estimated shipping costs.

❏ USE STRUCTURED DATA

Incorporate schema.org structured data into your site's code. Search engines use this data to better understand key elements of your products, and what information should be displayed in search results. Review all relevant structured data for products and incorporate all relevant information.

❏ DISPLAY PRODUCT AVAILABILITY

If you have a limited supply, showing the number of any product that you have in stock can be effective in persuading the visitor not to wait before buying. This is especially true when you are low on quantity. You also want to be sure to let your shoppers know when a product is out of stock or unavailable. If they can still place an order, let them know the expected delivery date if it is different from the norm.

❏ PROVIDE DELIVERY OPTIONS & DETAILS

Give your visitors multiple delivery options and the details of each. Some shoppers are willing to pay more for faster delivery, while others are content to wait a bit longer in order to save costs. Displaying multiple shipping options helps you meet every shopper's delivery needs.

❏ ESTIMATE DELIVERY DATE

During holiday seasons, delivery date estimation can help push the customer into making their purchase immediately so they get their order delivered in time. On normal days, however, it's still a good idea to provide an estimated delivery date on your product pages so your visitors have a general idea of when their orders will arrive.

❏ ADD SOCIAL BUTTONS

Give your visitors an opportunity to tell others about your products by adding social sharing buttons to each product page. When used, your product information will be broadcast to hundreds of other potential new customers in the shopper's social groups. You can also give visitors the opportunity to "like" a product, which can help reinforce the product's popularity.

❏ ADD SOCIAL META DATA

Several social networks, such as Twitter and Pinterest, allow greater detail to be displayed when your product pages are shared if proper meta data is implemented on your site. On Pinterest, for example, when a product page is pinned with rich pin data implemented on your site, real-time product availability and pricing is displayed on the pin. An email can be sent to the pinner when the price has dropped on the product they have pinned.

❏ ## LINK TO SITE SECURITY INFORMATION

Displaying your site security information in your global navigation is very smart. However, when you get to the product page level, additional information may be needed. Be sure to link to details of your site security and give your shoppers comfort in knowing their information is secure.

❏ ## PROVIDE RETURN & GUARANTEE INFO

Provide your visitors with information on your return and guarantee policies. If those policies are lengthy and won't fit on a product page, provide a link to a page that outlines all of this information in full. Even the presence of such a link can be enough to give the shopper the needed mental security to continue the shopping process.

❏ ## ALLOW "SAVE FOR LATER"

Not every shopper wants to buy a product right now. You can encourage them to come back later by providing an "add to wishlist" or "save for later" option. This allows them to save these products for viewing and purchase on their next visit. Wishlists often act as reminders for products the shopper may have forgotten they wanted, and ensures that if they do remember, they don't have to go hunting for it all over again.

❏ ## ALLOW "PRINT" OR "EMAIL THIS" OPTIONS

Some shoppers that are not quite ready to commit like having the option to print or email product information for review later, or to send it to a third party to buy. This is especially critical for B2B industries where there is regularly an additional person or persons that must provide final approval. Give your visitors options that keep them engaged with your site, and also the ability to pass your information along to others who may be in a position to buy.

❏ ## PRINTER-FRIENDLY PAGES

Create printer-friendly outputs for your product pages that allow the shopper to get a clean printout. This allows you to present your products in the most visually appealing format on paper, eliminating many of the things that are meant for the web, but useless on a printout.

❏ **RELATED PRODUCTS & UPSELLS**

Every product has a companion or something related that the buyer may be interested in as well. Helmets need goggles. Gloves need scarves. And those interested in Battlestar Galactica may also be interested in Firefly. Carve out an area of your product page to provide upsell information. This can be similar, related, popular, sale items or anything else you can conceive of. Any of these open the door for getting sales you might not have received otherwise.

❏ **INCLUDE PRODUCT REVIEWS**

Give visitors the option to read and submit their own product reviews. This user-generated content can be the best sales information on the entire product page. Many shoppers will simply not buy products that don't have at least a few user reviews. If you don't have this option, you are disenfranchising much of your buying audience. Don't be shy about including negative reviews, as this adds credibility to the positive ones.

❏ **PRODUCT COMPARISONS**

When you have a product with features or benefits that can easily be compared against those of another, provide a comparison option to help the shopper in the research and buying process. Allow shoppers to compare your product against competitor products, or even against other similar products on your own site.

❏ **OFFLINE COMPETITOR COMPARISON**

When competing against offline stores that allow the shopper to buy the same product(s) locally, you need to make the case why buying from you is better. There are many advantages to buying products offline. You need to overcome those with advantages of your own. You may not be able to beat "buy local," but you can offer other customer service options they can't get anywhere else.

❏ **PROVIDE RSS FEED**

Provide an RSS feed and/or social stream specifically for new product releases. This allows customers and brand lovers to be informed about new products, features or other information that might bring them back to buy again.

SHOPPING CART PAGE

One out of five abandonments is due, in part, to shoppers seized by security worries at the precise moment when you want them calmly clicking "buy." Why? Fears about identity theft. Spam. Hackers. In fact, many probably don't know why they're afraid, just that they are. The result is a lost sale.[19]

–McAfee

WHAT THIS CHECKLIST IS ABOUT

This checklist covers items pertaining to the actual shopping cart page where products are added before the shopper hits the "checkout" button to finalize their purchase. This checklist helps you close the holes in the shopping process, increase the number of visitors who complete their order, and prevent as many shoppers as possible from abandoning their purchase before the deal is done.

WHY YOUR SHOPPING CART PAGE IS IMPORTANT

When your goal is to get as many sales as possible, it's important to make sure your shoppers have the best shopping experience on your site as possible. That experience doesn't end in the aisles (i.e., product pages). It continues from there to the shopping cart page that collects all the items they "added to their cart" to purchase.

Unlike physical stores, it's not uncommon for visitors to abandon their shopping carts before they get to—or through—the checkout process. The reasons for this are many, and you will never be able to prevent it completely. Yet it's important to eliminate as many opportunities for cart abandonment as possible.

In sales, every little bit helps. Reducing your site and shopping cart abandonment rates can literally bring you thousands of dollars in increased sales without having to drive a single additional visitor to your site! Improving your shopping cart page will keep your visitors engaged throughout the entire sales process, boosting your online sales and success.

SHOPPING CART PAGE CHECKLIST

❏ OBVIOUS CHECKOUT LINK

This may seem like a no-brainer, but you might be surprised how many sites don't make their "checkout" button easy to find. Be sure that once in the shopping cart, the checkout button visually stands out from other elements on the page.

❏ INCLUDE PRODUCT THUMBNAILS

The shopping cart page should include a thumbnail image of each product that has been added to the cart. This allows the visitor to see all the products they are purchasing without having to read the text description of each one. Quick references such as these make shopping easier and speed up the checkout process, reducing opportunities for cart abandonment.

❏ BRIEF PRODUCT DESCRIPTIONS

Shoppers often review the products in their cart to ensure each is what they want. While you likely cannot provide a complete product description here, you can provide a two- or three-sentence description to accompany the actual product name. This ensures visitors are purchasing exactly what they want and don't have to navigate back out to each product page just to be sure.

❏ DISPLAY PRODUCT AVAILABILITY

At times, shoppers may be on the fence between buying a product now and waiting for later. Displaying the availability of the products in the cart can be effective in persuading the visitor to make the purchase immediately. If the visitor knows current supply is limited, the prospect of having to wait for it to become available again is often enough to keep the items in the cart as they checkout.

❑ ABILITY TO REMOVE ITEMS

Shoppers often add multiple items to their cart so they can sort through them later, deciding which to purchase. Customers should be able to easily remove items from their cart so they can move on to purchase the items they want. Not providing the ability to remove items only prompts the shopper to simply abandon the cart—and make the same purchase from someone else.

❑ UPDATABLE QUANTITIES

Shoppers should be able to increase or decrease the quantity of each item in their cart. Last-minute decisions may lead the shopper to wanting more (or less) than they initially thought. This option ensures they can purchase the correct number without the frustration of having to delete the product from the cart and go back to the product page to re-add it with the correct quantity.

❑ LINK TO PRODUCTS

Each item in the shopper's cart should link back to that item's product page. This allows the visitor to easily navigate back to the product details and re-read descriptions, features and benefits. This can be critical if the visitor is unsure if a product is exactly what they need, or if they are looking for more reassurances that it's right for them.

❑ PROVIDE PRODUCT AND TOTAL PRICE

Visitors don't make every decision on price alone, but it can be a powerful reinforcement. The shopping cart should include the price of each individual item, the quantity total of each product, the subtotal of all products in the cart, and current total for all items including tax.

❑ DISPLAY PAYMENT OPTIONS

Display all the payment options you accept near your checkout button. You want shoppers to know exactly what forms of payment they can (or can't) use as early in the checkout process as possible. If you don't accept a shopper's preferred payment option, it's better for them to know this sooner rather than later. No one wants to be the site that a visitor wasted an hour of their life on!

❏ COUPONS & VOUCHERS EXPLAINED

If you offer discount coupons, vouchers or other payment options, provide a place on the shopping cart page for this information to be entered or selected. Provide this before the visitor begins to checkout so they can see any cost adjustments before going further.

❏ SECURITY ASSURANCES

When collecting credit card or other personal information, be sure to provide and link to your security reassurances. Links to privacy policies, secure shopping information and even product return guarantees can provide much needed comfort to new customers.

❏ LINK TO GUARANTEES

If you offer any guarantees regarding delivery, product quality, returns, etc., the shopping cart is a great place to provide those links for your customers. Most visitors won't follow them, but as with most guarantees, just the fact they are present can give the visitor added security and feelings of trust in doing business with you.

❏ SHOW DELIVERY COSTS

Even if you provide multiple delivery options to choose from later in the process, provide the shopper with as much delivery cost detail as possible. Let them know their expected (even if estimated) shipping costs so they can make a fully informed purchase decision.

❏ ESTIMATE DELIVERY DATE

Provide shoppers with an estimated delivery date based on standard shipping times. Visitors should have the option to select faster (or slower) shipping options later, but before moving further into the purchase process, shoppers should be able to see when they could expect to receive their items.

❏ ANSWER SHIPPING & RETURN QUESTIONS

Provide (or link to) answers to typical shipping and return questions. This is a point of concern for many online shoppers who might otherwise find the same product at a local store. Make shoppers feel as if your return process is as easy as any brick-and-mortar competitor.

❏ INTERNATIONAL SHIPPING OPTIONS

Be sure to let international shoppers know their purchase and shipping options, including additional expenses incurred, if any, before going any further in the check-out process. If you do not provide international shipping, be sure shoppers are aware of this early.

❏ DISPLAY CONTACT INFORMATION

Some shoppers may have last-minute questions that need to be answered before committing to their purchase. Provide an avenue for the shopper to contact you to get these questions answered immediately, and even complete their order over the phone if necessary. Providing a point of contact can be an easy way to persuade the shopper to complete their purchase more quickly!

❏ PROVIDE RELATED PRODUCT / UPSELL OPTIONS

You can discreetly provide last-minute upsell options, especially for products that might be related, desired or even essential to the products already in the cart. Don't go overboard (show only a few items at a time) and choose products wisely for maximum upsell impact.

❏ "CONTINUE SHOPPING" LINK

Don't lock your visitors into the shopping cart with no way back to shop for more items. Shoppers often start the checkout process before realizing there is something else they want or need. Give them the option to navigate back to your products; preferably sending them to the last page they were on before clicking into the shopping cart.

❏ NO UNNECESSARY NAVIGATIONAL ELEMENTS

Limiting your visitor's options for leaving the checkout page can be good for business, forcing them to continue through the conversion process. Greatly reduce—or even eliminate—your traditional navigation on the cart page. However, be sure not to prevent them from moving back to products should they want to do additional shopping.

❏ BLOCK FROM SEARCH ENGINES

Search engines do not need to spider or index your shopping cart page. Use whatever available methods you have to ensure that the cart page does not end up in the search engines' indexes. The best solution is to prevent the page from being spidered altogether. (See Site Architectural Issues)

❏ PROVIDE MINICARTS

Let your visitors see the products they are adding to their cart as they're being added. Don't force them into the shopping cart page every time a new product is added. This gives the visitor a more seamless shopping experience without forcing unnecessary navigating.

MINICART

A page needs focus for people to understand what
it is you want. On the checkout page this is doubly
true; if your focus isn't on the process of checking
out, people will get confused. And confused people
don't convert.[20]

–Joost de Valk
Yoast

WHAT THIS CHECKLIST IS ABOUT

Many ecommerce sites provide a minicart, either as an overlay or on the side (or top) of the
page being viewed. This allows visitors to see items being added to their cart as they are
added, along with product quantities and even total price without having to go to the full
cart page. This list covers these minicarts so you can give shoppers maximum value during
their online shopping experience.

WHY MINICARTS ARE IMPORTANT

Minicarts provide a visual display for shoppers to know how many products they have
added to their cart, what those products are, and/or the total dollar amount of their order
thus far. This helps them keep track of their order without being forced into the shopping
cart page every time they add a new product, or having to click into another page to get an
up-to-date view of their intended purchases.

These minicarts come in many forms: Some are ever-present on the side or top of the page,
others might be a quick overlay that can be accessed with a simple mouse-over, and still
others might only provide small pieces of information, such as a total number of products

currently in the cart. While these minicarts are not designed to replace the shopping cart page, you can take full advantage of your on-page real estate to give your shoppers a better shopping experience.

Providing shoppers with as much information as possible in a minicart reduces the number of clicks they have to take on your site, creating a more seamless shopping experience. Utilize these overlays to keep the visitors engaged with the shopping process. This prevents interruptions and excessive clicking that increases time on the site unnecessarily and often leads to cart abandonment.

MINICART CHECKLIST

❑ NEWLY ADDED PRODUCTS ARE OBVIOUS

When visitors click an "add to cart" button, make sure they know it was successfully added, without forcing them to go into the shopping cart page itself. This can be accomplished with a simple pop up message or by having the new product appear in an already visible minicart.

❑ LINK TO FULL CART/CHECKOUT PAGE

Since minicarts cannot (and should not) provide the full checkout page experience, be sure to provide a link to "view cart" or "checkout" right from this display area. This link should be clear and obvious to the shopper's eye.

❑ ALLOW REMOVAL OF PRODUCTS

Visitors should be able to remove products right from the minicart. It's helpful, though not necessary, to allow shoppers to increase or decrease the quantity in the minicart. If necessary, they can do that in the full cart page. However, removal of products is important to keep the information displayed as accurate as possible.

❑ PROVIDE ORDER TOTAL

Calculate all product costs and provide a current checkout total, including shipping and tax if applicable. Let the visitor know exactly what the cost will be should they move on to the checkout process.

CHECKOUT PROCESS

67.45% of online shopping carts are abandoned. Think about that. For every 100 potential customers, 67 of them will leave without purchasing.[21]

–Michael Zipursky
Consulting Success

WHAT THIS CHECKLIST IS ABOUT

This list covers the actual process of checking out and paying for products on your website. After products are added and visitors review the items in their cart, they are then directed to "checkout" and purchase the items. The items in this list cover the process from hitting "checkout," to the shopper receiving the final order confirmation.

WHY THE CHECKOUT PROCESS IS IMPORTANT

Getting your visitors to add products to your shopping cart is good, but it's not a win. If you want a sales victory, you have to get shoppers to commit to purchasing the products they added to the cart, without abandoning it before the purchase is complete as many shoppers do.

If the checkout process on your site is confusing, tedious or annoys the shopper in any way, you are opening yourself up to the possibility of losing them before they complete their purchase. The goal is to provide a quick and seamless process for checking out that eliminates as many abandonment points as possible.

The fewer checkout barriers you have, the less likely you are to lose the sale before it's complete. Streamlining your checkout process is critical. In fact, improvements to your checkout process can increase sales considerably without having to drive even one additional visitor to your site.

CHECKOUT PROCESS CHECKLIST

❏ ## SECURE CHECKOUT

If your entire site isn't secure, your checkout page (and beyond) must be. This is where shoppers will be adding sensitive information such as personal contact info, credit card numbers and more. This information must be locked down behind HTTPS security.

❏ ## DON'T REQUIRE PRE-REGISTRATION

Visitors don't like to be made to create an account just to make a purchase. If possible, allow shoppers to purchase as a guest. However, if registration must be required, add that to the very end rather than the beginning of the checkout process. Once they have all but completed checking out, the only step left should be to add a password.

❏ ## SHOW CC AND SECURITY INFO

The checkout process is one of the most critical places to show which credit cards you accept along with other site security information. Be sure to place this information in an obvious place to encourage visitors to continue their shopping experience.

❏ ## NO HIDDEN FEES

Don't add additional fees that are shown only after the visitor commits to the purchase. All fees and costs should be explained before the visitor ever hits the "checkout" button. Any changes to pricing beyond this point will not only cause you to lose the sale, you'll very possibly lose the customer, possibly ¬for life.

❏ ## SHOW CHECKOUT PROGRESS METER

When you have multiple steps in your checkout process, show a progress meter that allows shoppers to see how many steps there are. As shoppers move from one stage to the next, the progress meter should show progress along the way so each visitor knows exactly where they are in the process, and how many more steps remain until their order is finalized.

❏ KEEP CHECKOUT PROCESS SHORT

Eliminate as many checkout steps as possible. Using a single form and reducing the amount of information required can be critical to streamlining your checkout processes. The fewer steps required, the fewer opportunities you give your visitors to leave before they finalize their purchase. Ideally, you want no more than three to five steps in the entire checkout process.

❏ INTERNATIONAL ADDRESS FORMS

If you ship internationally, be sure your checkout forms allow for the nuances of international addresses, phone numbers, zip codes and the like. Many international orders can be lost if it isn't clear to the visitor where their country-specific information goes.

❏ ALLOW GIFT OPTIONS

Many shoppers buy gifts for friends and family. You can assist them by allowing shoppers to mark items as gifts that then get treated differently from the rest of the order. Provide options for gift wrapping and shipping to a separate address. Adding an option to include a custom card is a nice additional touch.

❏ PROVIDE REGISTRATION BENEFITS

When registration becomes necessary, don't just expect visitors to be okay with you keeping their personal information in your database. Give reasons why registration is necessary, and list the benefits they receive when they create an account with you.

Some benefits you might expand upon include:
- ❏ FASTER CHECKOUT IN FUTURE
- ❏ ACCESS TO ORDER HISTORY
- ❏ CHECK ORDER STATUS ANYTIME
- ❏ "SAVE" OR "WISHLIST" OPTION
- ❏ ACCESS TO PROMOTIONS
- ❏ PERSONALIZED EXPERIENCE
- ❏ JOINING THE COMMUNITY

❏ Don't Keep Personal Info Unless Authorized

Be sure that you don't keep any of your shopper's personal information unless they specifically authorize you to do so when they create an account. If you allow visitors to buy as a "guest," assure them that their credit card, address, phone number, or any other personal info will not be kept.

❏ Receipt/Order Confirmation

After the order is submitted, provide a receipt and a confirmation of each item ordered. This allows your customers to have a printable receipt for future reference, along with the total cost for their records.

Here are some items that should be included in your order confirmation:

❏ Thank You Message

The initial order confirmation should contain a message of thanks. Let your customers know how valuable they are to you.

❏ Order Confirmation Number

The order receipt should contain a confirmation number that the shopper can use to follow up on the order, refer back to if changes need to be made, or make a correction if an error occurred.

❏ Order Date

Provide the date on which the order was placed. This is primarily for the shopper's recordkeeping and is valuable information if they need to refer back to any particular order in the future.

❏ List Items Purchased

The confirmation should list all of the items purchased, providing brief descriptions and costs associated with each.

❏ EXPECTED DELIVERY DATE

Let the visitor know when they can expect delivery of their order. If items will be shipped over multiple dates, be sure to let them know when they can expect each item to arrive.

❏ NOTE METHOD OF PAYMENT

Upon looking back at the order, shoppers may not remember how they paid or what credit card was used. Note their method of payment for handy reference.

❏ AFTER-SALE GUARANTEES

Provide (or link to) information regarding customer satisfaction policies (guarantees, return policies, etc.), as well as any warranty information the shopper will want to have a record of.

❏ CANCELLATION POLICY

Provide (or link to) your cancellation policy information. Be sure this includes the process the shopper must follow if they choose to cancel the order.

❏ RETURN POLICY

Provide (or link to) your return policies. This should include information on how to start the return process for any particular item in their order. Be sure to address the costs associated with the return of any item. For best usability, provide a link with each item ordered that the visitor can use to start the return process.

❏ PRINTABLE

Web-based receipts should be in a printer-friendly format that allows the visitor to keep a hard copy for their records.

❏ EMAILED

Email a copy of the order (and all of the information above) to the shopper as an alternate means of recordkeeping, and for easy reference to ensure all items get delivered.

❏ AFTER-ORDER FOLLOW-UP

The end of one sale is just the beginning of the next. Be sure to follow up with your shoppers after the order is placed. Give your visitors further information on order status, when items have shipped, expected delivery (once shipped) and even promotions for their next purchase.

LOGIN & ACCOUNT PAGES

88% of people have intentionally left website registration information blank or inserted false information. Whether it's due to privacy concerns or frustration, online shoppers have higher standards than ever before for a sleek and simple registration process.[22]

–Corey Eridon
HubSpot

WHAT THIS CHECKLIST IS ABOUT

This list covers items that have to do with the process of how your visitors log in to your site or access account information they have saved. This is not exclusive of ecommerce sites, but for any site that incorporates a registration option, or provides options for visitors to log in to access certain information.

WHY LOGIN & ACCOUNT PAGES ARE IMPORTANT

Many sites offer members-only access to certain information, or require visitors to create accounts in order to enjoy the full benefits of what they offer. Ensuring visitors can log in easily and quickly is a necessary part of improving the on-site experience for your members; however, it is only the first hurdle.

Once logged in to your system, your visitors need to be able to edit their profile and personal information with relative ease. Sites that make editing personal information difficult or cumbersome are apt to lose members of their community.

In addition, visitors with login accounts must be confident that their private information is secure, and that they maintain the ability to edit or remove any personal information as needed. Without these assurances, your visitors may feel that their data is, or may be, used improperly or perhaps isn't as secure as it should be. Use the following action points to create a more seamless process for improving your login and account pages.

LOGIN & ACCOUNT PAGE CHECKLIST

❏ EASY-TO-FIND LOGIN

If you want your visitors to log in to your site, make sure that they can easily find the login link. It should be available from any page on the site and in an obvious location so the visitor does not have to hunt for it. The most likely place for this is in the top navigation.

❏ LOGGED-IN STATUS

With just a glance, visitors should be able to tell whether or not they are logged in. This should be noted around the same area where the login link is placed on the site.

❏ EASY LOGOUT

Allow the visitor to log out with a simple click of a link. This link should be in the immediate vicinity of the logged-in status indicator.

❏ USE SECURITY PROTOCOLS

Be sure to keep the user's data secure at all times using strict security protocols for hosting and authenticating their information. If visitors feel as if their information isn't secure, many will simply not engage with your site—and they certainly won't be inclined to give you their personal information.

❏ PROVIDE SECURITY ASSURANCES

Aside from maintaining strict security protocols, it is also important to let the visitor know how their information will be stored. Provide links and information regarding your security protocols for the visitor to read at their convenience.

❑ **LINK FOR NEW REGISTRATIONS**

Don't just have a login page. Allow visitors to choose between logging in and registering to join your community. To get as many visitors as possible to sign up, the registration form information must be easy to find and fill out.

❑ **PROVIDE BENEFITS OF JOINING**

Don't assume visitors will automatically want to join your community. The new registrations page should outline the benefits of signing up. Give them as many reasons as you can.

❑ **RECOVER/RESET PASSWORD OPTION**

Losing or forgetting passwords happens far more frequently than many people realize. Provide a way for visitors to recover or reset their password. This ensures they continue to stay engaged with the community rather than just abandoning it all together.

❑ **"REMEMBER ME" OPTION**

Don't force visitors to enter their username and password each time they come to your site. Give them the option to stay logged in for long periods of time. Allow participants to select a "keep me logged in" option that won't force a logout until they have not returned to the site for at least several weeks. Even once the system does log them out, it's helpful to keep their username entered so they only need to input their password to continue.

❑ **CHANGE OF INFO CONFIRMATION**

When a member's personal information is changed, send a change confirmation email. If the action wasn't authorized, this email allows them to know their account has been compromised.

❑ **LINK TO PRIVACY POLICY**

Provide a link to your privacy policy information. This gives your members security in knowing how their private information will be handled and protected.

❏ METHOD OF DELIVERY OPTIONS

Items can be delivered in all kinds of ways: Products can be shipped fast or slow, PDFs can be sent to your inbox or iPad, and emails can be delivered in text or HTML format. Let your members set a standard method of delivery that best suits their needs.

❏ LINK TO FINANCIAL INFORMATION

Provide a way for your members to access their financial information and transactions. This allows them to review at any time for verification purposes.

Here are some items that members should have access to:

❏ TRANSACTION HISTORY

Allow visitors to see a history of all their orders or transactions, including dates and amounts. This helps them reconcile issues with their bank and ensures that no documentation mistakes were made.

❏ INVOICES

Visitors should be able to go back and review their past invoices along with all items purchased in each transaction.

❏ ACCOUNT BALANCES

If your members have ongoing payments and debits, keep detailed records. This information should be accessible for review at any time.

❏ DEFAULT PAYMENT METHODS

Members should be able to review, set and change their default payment method. They should have no problem adding/removing credit cards, updating associated address info, etc.

FORMS AND ERROR MESSAGES

> Error messages have a bigger impact on form completion rates than most think. Don't make the mistake of ignoring your error messages, or you'll find users leaving your website for another one.[23]
>
> —Anthony T.
> UX Movement

WHAT THIS CHECKLIST IS ABOUT

This checklist covers the all-important web form and corresponding error messages that occur when a form entry mistake is made. It covers items designed to create the most user-friendly forms and form fields possible to ensure that this final conversion step is completed without a hitch.

WHY FORMS AND ERROR MESSAGES ARE IMPORTANT

Forms are a standard method of allowing visitors to communicate with you directly from your website. They are often the final hurdle the visitor has to overcome before they have completed their tasks on your website. As such, it is imperative that your web forms function properly, or else you risk visitor abandonment when you were thisclose to getting the completion!

Website forms can be used for simple things such as emailing your company, downloading a document, or for more complex issues such as placing an order on your website. When forms don't function to a visitor's satisfaction, your site abandonment rates will climb. When forms function correctly, you'll see an increase in form completions and "conversions."

Because even simple forms can be quite complex, there are a lot of things that can go wrong. Many times, the problems may not even be visible, but occur behind the scenes once information is submitted. Other times problems can occur by poor programming of the form fields or how the data should be entered. There is a lot of room for error here—both on the programming and user end—and getting the programming correct from the start is critical.

Even the most basic forms can produce errors, and when something goes wrong, the message presented to your visitors is just as important as the form itself. Bad, insulting or confusing error messaging can be that final roadblock to what would have been an otherwise successful online journey.

FORMS & ERROR MESSAGE CHECKLIST

❏ CLEARLY LABELED FIELDS

Be sure the label for each field is clearly identified and the visitor knows precisely what information is required. Don't allow room for any ambiguity. Make clear which fields are required and how specific data is to be entered.

❏ TEXT LABEL ABOVE FIELD

It's common practice for web developers to put the text label on the left of the field entry box. However, for better usability, you should place the text label above the field input. This allows visitors using small screens, such as smartphones, to fill out the form without additional side-to-side scrolling. It's also helpful for those with visual impairments to know exactly which labels go with which fields.

❏ PLACEHOLDER TEXT REMOVED

If you use placeholder text within any form fields, that text must disappear once the user begins to add data. Keep in mind that you should never use form field labels as placeholder text. The visitor should always be able to see the purpose of each field. When field labels are implemented as placeholder text, it's easy for the user to forget the purpose of the field

❏ STACK FIELDS VERTICALLY

Even as computer monitors are getting wider, allowing you to fit more information horizontally on the screen, it's a good idea to stack all your form fields into a single vertical column. This prevents information from being missed on monitors that may not be as wide or on narrower mobile devices.

❏ PRE-FILL CONTENT

When possible, pre-fill the form content based on user data. For example, let the visitor enter a zip code first so the city, state and country information can be automatically populated. The same can be done when visitors click tracking or coupon links, etc. Also, attempt to pull information from the device itself to pre-populate any forms to make submission as easy as possible.

❏ FLEXIBLE FIELD ENTRY

Allow maximum flexibility for visitors entering their information into forms. The more flexibility you offer, the less entry errors will happen, ensuring visitors reach their goals with minimal frustration.

Phone Number Entry Examples
Yes: 123-456-7890
Yes: 1234567890
Yes: 123 456 7890
Yes: (123) 456-7890
Yes: +1 (123)467789

❏ CAN TAB BETWEEN FIELDS

Set your forms so visitors can hit the tab key to move from field to field. Be sure the fields are set in order so each tab takes them to the next subsequent field rather than jumping all over the form. This functionality allows visitors to quickly move through the form without forcing them back to their mouse to move to the next input field.

❏ REQUEST ONLY NECESSARY INFO

It's tempting to use your forms to collect as much information as you can. However, the more information that you request in each form (regardless of whether it's required or not), the less likely visitors are to fill it out. Keep the forms slim and ask for only what you need, with few—if any—embellishments.

❏ MINIMAL INSTRUCTIONS

Keep instructions for filling out forms and specific fields as minimalistic as possible. Most visitors do not read instructions, so make the form work as intuitively as possible without them.

❏ INSTRUCTIONS ABOVE THE FIELD

When instructions for filling out a particular form field are necessary, place the instructions below the text label but above the form field itself. This ensures visitors are more likely to read them before filling out the field.

❏ PRE-SELECTED FIELD OPTIONS

When applicable for any particular field, provide visitors with a list of options to choose from rather than requiring them to type in their response. This is great for specific categorization requirements, state or country selections and other types of data where there are a limited number of correct responses. While this requires additional programming, the increased usability will manifest itself with fewer input errors to correct later.

❏ COMPREHENSIVE CHOICES

If you provide a list of selections for a particular field, be sure the options are comprehensive enough for all visitors. For example, offering a list of states to select from works great for US visitors, but not for those from other countries. Or, if visitors are selecting a business industry, be sure your pre-made options cover all occupations sufficiently.

❏ APPROPRIATE FIELD SIZE

Input fields should be sized appropriately for the amount of information that is requested. Don't make the fields so narrow that it causes the information to move out of the visible area as visitors type. The only exception is for large text fields where some vertical scrolling may be necessary. Leave room for at least a couple of paragraphs to be displayed before scrolling begins.

❏ PROPER USE OF BUTTONS AND BOXES

Use the proper field for the type of information you are gathering. If you want the visitor to make multiple selections from several options, use a checkbox field before each option. However, if you want the visitor to select only one option, use a radio button so no more than one option can be selected at a time.

❏ ANNOTATE REQUIRED FIELDS

When specific fields are required, be sure to indicate this both visually and textually. Make it clear to the visitor which fields must be completed so they can be sure to fill it in before the form is submitted. Usually a red asterisk with a note above the first field is a strong enough indicator.

> **Example**
> *Indicates required field*

❏ NO AUTOCOMPLETE ON SENSITIVE FIELDS

Autocomplete is a nice option for a lot of routine information; however, there are some fields that should not be autocompleted. Fields for passwords, credit card information and other sensitive data should not allow autofill to be used without the visitor's express consent.

❏ USE MULTI-STEP FORMS

Some studies show that multi-step forms actually help visitors commit to completing the process as they don't want to abandon a form they have already invested multiple steps into completing. If you have a lot of required form fields, break the form into multiple pages with the most important information in the first step(s). Leave the non-essential information for later pages/steps. At the very least, you'll have their most important information already submitted even if they don't complete the remaining steps. One thing to keep in mind is that long forms have a larger abandonment rate than short forms.

❑ PROGRESS INDICATOR

If your form spans multiple pages, include some form of progress indicator so visitors can see how many pages or questions remain. This reduces form abandonment rates by letting the visitors see exactly where they are in the process and how soon the task of completing the form will be done.

Examples
Page 2 of 3
Question 24/30

❑ BACK NAVIGATION

When visitors submit one page of a form and move to the next, give them the ability to navigate back to previously answered form questions. Visitors who feel that a previous answer was inadequate need to be able to correct it. Otherwise they are faced with the options of submitting improper data, starting over, or abandoning the form completely. None of these are helpful to the visitor—or to your business.

❑ SUBMIT BUTTON CLOSE TO FIELDS

Place the form submission button close to the data being submitted. Don't allow too much space between the entry fields and the final "submit" button, or push the button off to the side where it's difficult to spot. Keep input fields and the submission buttons in the same visual space so it's clear they all belong together.

❑ SUBMIT BUTTON NOTES ACTION

The submit button should use words that tell the visitor what action clicking the button will accomplish. Words such as "place order," "go to" or "download now" are great for enticing visitors to take the desired action, knowing the exact, immediate result. Words such as "submit" are vague, and don't convey any urgency to the visitor to complete the form submission process.

Examples
No: *Submit*
Yes: *Add to Cart*
Yes: *Download Ebook*
Yes: *Complete Purchase*

❏ No "Reset" or "Cancel" Option

Don't allow visitors to reset already-filled-out form fields or to cancel out of the form altogether. While this may sound like good usability, more often than not, these buttons are hit accidentally, erasing all of the previously inputted information. Yes, it's the visitor's own fault, but it's stupid to make it easy for visitors to do something so stupid!

❏ Preserve Entered Data

If visitors err when filling out a form, be sure to preserve all the data already completed. The form should not reset, requiring the visitor to type in all the information again. They should only be required to fix the particular where the error occurred.

❏ Friendly Error Output

Error messages that appear when a form is filled out incorrectly should use friendly, helpful language. Don't create messages that blame the visitor, but rather help them fix the error. Error messages that are anything less than polite may dissuade the visitor from fixing the error and completing the form submission.

Examples
No: *"You did something wrong."*
Yes: *"Oops, that doesn't appear to be a valid email address."*

❏ Errors Describe Remedy

Error messages should provide usable instructions that give visitors whatever information they need to correct the issue.

Examples
No: *"You didn't enter the phone number correctly."*
Yes: *"Please enter the phone number as xxx-xxx-xxxx"*

❏ Errors Obviously Indicated

Be sure to clearly highlight the fields in which the errors occurred. This allows visitors to quickly find and fix the problem with minimum hunting, without the frustration that occurs when they have trouble locating the right field to correct.

❏ PROVIDE CONTACT OPTION

Some errors are not the fault of the user but rather the form's programmers. Be sure to include a way for visitors to contact you and notify you of the problem. If visitors are unable to submit a form due to a programming error, they will usually just leave. Providing a contact option gives someone a chance to let you know why so few people are filling out your form.

> **Example**
> *Having trouble with this form? Call us now so we can help you out.*

❏ REMOVE SITE NAVIGATION

When a form is spread out over multiple pages, it can be a good idea to remove the site's main navigation. This keeps visitors focused on the task and reduces their ability to leave before the form is complete. Use navigation primarily to get your visitors through the form process rather than out of it.

❏ LINK TO PRIVACY INFORMATION

If your form is used for collecting personal data, be sure to provide a link to your privacy policies. These links provide valuable reassurances for visitors so they can be confident that their personal information will not be abused.

❏ FINAL VERIFICATION

Once the form is completely filled out and submitted, provide a confirmation screen that details all the information entered. Give visitors the opportunity to go back and correct any inaccurate information before the data's final submission.

❏ CONFIRMATION PAGE

Once the form submission process is complete, provide the visitor with a confirmation message that the information was received. Depending on the form, it can be a good idea to give the visitor an idea of what they can expect next (i.e. when products will be shipped, when they will get a call, etc.).

THANK YOU /
CONFIRMATION PAGES

Thank You pages are more than just a mechanism to show appreciation for a purchase or downloading a piece of content. A well-planned Thank You page can be a powerful tool for cross-selling, gathering lead intelligence, sharing content and expanding your social reach.[24]

–Shannon Fuldauer
Kuno Creative

WHAT THIS CHECKLIST IS ABOUT

Confirmation or Thank You pages are not exclusively for ecommerce sites. They are relevant to any site that has a submission form, and/or offers an online download to visitors. The points in this list will ensure the end of the initial transaction isn't the end of the conversion, but the beginning of the next one.

WHY CONFIRMATION PAGES ARE IMPORTANT

We all know that it costs more to get a new customer than it does to keep an existing one. That means that what you do after the form is submitted (to complete an order, contact you, download a PDF, etc.) is even more valuable than what happened before they got to that point.

A poorly crafted confirmation page tells your visitors nothing more than that their form submission went through. However, if you take the time to create a thoughtful and focused confirmation page, you're telling your visitors how valuable they are to your business.

Rather than ending the relationship with the customer once the sale is complete, you're prepping them for the next interaction—which is hopefully taking the step toward a future conversion.

In effect, you're using the confirmation page to begin earning future business from this "old" customer. It's not just about saying "thanks," but about providing value back to your visitor and showing appreciation for their feedback, download, or purchase. Keep them hooked on your site, and you keep a customer; keep them engaged after they've taken a form action, and you keep a customer for life.

CONFIRMATION PAGE CHECKLIST

❑ ADDRESS VISITORS BY NAME

One of the pieces of information forms often ask for is the visitor's name. Who says you have to wait for some future follow-up message before you can use it? Start now by addressing each submitter by name on both your confirmation page and email.

Example
John, thanks for downloading our ebook. We hope you find it valuable to growing your business!

❑ SAY "THANKS"

We can sometimes get so caught up in what we want our confirmation pages to achieve that we forget the most important thing: Actually saying, "Thank you!" The importance of these two words cannot be understated.

Example
Thank you, John, for your business. Please come back soon as our inventory is always growing!

❏ CONFIRM TRANSACTION

Whether the visitor bought a product, requested information or downloaded an ebook, be sure to provide confirmation that the transaction is complete. As necessary, reiterate what it was they received, what charges there were (if any), and when they will receive the product, information, or follow up they requested.

Example
John, thanks for downloading our Best Damn Web Marketing Cheat Sheet! It will be delivered to your email shortly.

❏ LINK TO NEXT ACTIONS

By virtue of the form submission, you now have a "customer" who likes what you offer. Now is the time to offer something more that they might be interested in. This could be related products, additional information or more resources. If they downloaded free content, you can offer them something they might pay for, or vice versa. Look at your options and upsell your visitors on the next best thing.

Example
... in the meantime, check out our ebook library for more great information to help you grow your business!

❏ REFERENCE NUMBER

Be sure to include some kind of reference number in case there is a problem with the fulfillment of the visitor's transaction. This can be an order, transaction, customer or other reference number the visitor will use to help you track each particular form submission.

❏ EXPECTED DELIVERY/TRACKING

If products are to be delivered, be sure to include the expected delivery date(s) as well as shipment tracking information. If you don't have specific tracking numbers available immediately, let your visitors know that you will send them once available, along with the necessary links.

❏ POLICY INFORMATION

If there is any policy information relevant to the submitter's request, be sure to include a link to the necessary details. Anything by way of warrantees, guarantees, cancellation and return policies are important for the visitor to have.

❏ TESTIMONIALS

Use testimonials to give visitors reassurance that the transaction they just completed was a wise one. This provides valuable encouragement to come back and continue interacting with your company. Provide a handful of brief testimonials from real people, with a link to more testimonials for their reading pleasure.

❏ SOCIAL SHARING OPTIONS

Encourage your visitors to share their purchase/download/transaction on Twitter, Facebook, LinkedIn or other applicable network. This is their chance to share their interest and excitement, while giving your company a promotional boost as well.

❏ OPTION TO CREATE ACCOUNT

If creating an account isn't necessary before the form is submitted, the confirmation page provides a great opportunity to encourage your visitors to do so. Depending on how much information was gathered in the form, very little additional information will likely be required, such as creating a password to make future purchases that much easier. It's a small hurdle, and if you provide benefits of creating an account, you're sure to get quite a few takers.

❏ EMAIL OPT-IN/AUTORESPONDERS

Give your visitors an opportunity to join your mailing list for more information, benefits, tips or deals. Don't automatically sign them up; always be sure to ask their permission first. Once granted, have some autoresponders in place for automated follow up via email. While typically this option is presented before the form is submitted, it is often better to provide this option after.

❏ SURVEY/FEEDBACK

If you want to get feedback or testimonials from your visitors, or would like them to take a survey, now is the time to ask. Provide a call to action within a link and be sure to keep the feedback process as simple as possible.

❏ EMAILED

Email a copy of the information on the confirmation page to your visitors as an alternate means of recordkeeping. This also provides visitors with another chance to take you up on the next call to action.

❏ PRINTABLE

Be sure the confirmation page is printable. It must print cleanly without any unnecessary information on the page. This printout will be used by many visitors for their records, or for any necessary follow up.

❏ KEEP FROM SEARCH ENGINES

Search engines should not have access to your confirmation pages. You don't want these pages to be indexed or for search engines to provide a link to them in any way. Review the architecture considerations section to see how best to keep these pages hidden.

HELP & FAQ PAGES

Your FAQ page represents one of the most valuable moments in a conversion funnel. Nowhere else does a visitor so deliberately indicate that they want to know the details of your product or service.[25]

—Jason Shah
KISSmetrics

WHAT THIS CHECKLIST IS ABOUT

This list covers a range of items dealing with pages dedicated to helping your visitors find what they want and answering important questions. While this is not a large checklist, it does contain key elements that are specific to ensuring your visitors stay engaged with your site until they find whatever information they need to complete their goals.

WHY HELP & FAQ PAGES ARE IMPORTANT

Help and FAQ pages are often rarely visited; nevertheless, they are critical pages to incorporate into your site. While not every site will need both pages, it's a good idea to provide answers to typical questions visitors ask about your products or services. These pages will hopefully spare you calls or emails by making sure answers to common questions are already easily accessible on your site.

When visitors start digging through your help and FAQ pages, chances are they are looking for information that isn't provided elsewhere on your site. Or at least in a place they can find it. While it's best to answer as many of your visitor's questions within the main site pages, it can't always be done. Providing access to help and FAQ pages can keep visitors engaged with your site as they keep learning more about what you offer. When done right, your help and FAQ pages will be a valuable asset in pushing your visitors through to the next stage in the conversion process.

HELP & FAQ PAGE CHECKLIST

❏ LINK TO ADDITIONAL PAGES

While you want to answer questions directly in your help and FAQ pages, you can provide additional benefit to your visitors by linking to other areas of the site. This is especially true if you have pages that provide greater detail for any particular topic.

Here are some helpful resources worth linking to:
- ❏ USER GUIDES
- ❏ DOWNLOADS
- ❏ CONTACT US/ABOUT US PAGES
- ❏ TECHNICAL DATA/SPECIFICATIONS
- ❏ PRODUCT SUPPORT
- ❏ RESOURCE LIBRARY
- ❏ CUSTOMER SUPPORT

❏ LINK TO OUTSIDE RESOURCES

There are times when your site cannot provide complete answers or discuss a particular topic in the amount of detail required. Sometimes you may need to reinforce your answers with outside resources. In these instances, link out to the external sources that provide your visitors with the additional information they need. The more helpful you are to your visitors—even to the point of sending them to another website—the more credibility you'll have as the "solution source."

Example
For more checklists on web marketing, check out Pole Position Marketing's Best Damn Web Marketing Cheat Sheet!

❑ INTERNAL HELP SEARCH

If your help pages are robust, your visitors may not be able to easily find what they are looking for with a quick scan. Be sure your internal site search includes all help and FAQ pages in the search results. Even better, provide an option that allows visitors to narrow their search to these pages specifically.

❑ PRINTABLE TEXT

This issue has been addressed previously, but it bears repeating, especially for robust help and FAQ pages: Allow your visitors to print whatever specific information they need, being sure that the printed text is in a readable format for offline viewing.

PRIVACY & SECURITY PAGES

Privacy policies are often not given the attention they deserve. Many companies churn them out, not realizing their true importance. While not everyone will read the policy, it's these types of policies that say a lot about what the company stands for and what it wants to achieve.[26]

–Sara Hawkins
Social Media Examiner

WHAT THIS CHECKLIST IS ABOUT

This list covers items for the pages on your site that outline your company's privacy policy and how your visitor's personal information is handled once submitted to you. It provides key information to ensure that your visitors get what they need and that information is presented in a way that allows them to find the reassurances they seek.

WHY PRIVACY & SECURITY PAGES ARE IMPORTANT

While most visitors won't read—much less even visit—your privacy or security pages, they do provide necessary assurances that visitors typically look for in a site they want to do business with. In most cases, the visitor will be happy with nothing more than seeing a clear link to either (or both) of these pages. However, the content of these pages is critical for those visitors who do click the link, regardless if they read the page(s) in full or not.

Once your visitor navigates to either of these pages, they are there to find assurances of your trustworthiness with their personal information. What information you provide and how you present it to them is important in order to provide these visitors with the reassurance they seek.

PRIVACY & SECURITY PAGE CHECKLIST

❏ LINKED IN FOOTER

Your footer is a great place to add links (or a link) to your privacy and security page(s). A link there is always out of the way, while also being consistently accessible.

❏ EASY-TO-READ FORMAT

Privacy and security pages are typically written as "small print" that you hope is never read. Instead, these pages should be written as any other helpful content on your site. Treat these pages as all others, organizing them so they are easy to read, scan and digest.

❏ SUMMARIZE SECTIONS

If your privacy and security pages are long and/or have many content sections, it can be helpful to summarize each section before diving into the full content. This helps readers to get the "gist" of what a more detailed read will provide, and allows them to skip it (if they so choose) while still getting a basic understanding of the content.

❏ PROVIDE CONSUMER PROTECTION TUTORIALS

Including consumer protection content is a great opportunity to provide additional articles, information and tutorials that your visitors will appreciate. Such tutorials let your visitors know you are looking out for their best interests and give them even more confidence in doing business with you.

❑ ## LINK TO CONTACT INFO

While your contact information should be easy to find in your main navigation, providing detailed contact information on privacy and security pages adds additional confidence and assurances. In short, it lets your visitors know you are available for questions or comments regarding this data specifically, should they have any.

❑ ## IDENTIFY INFORMATION YOU COLLECT

Let your visitors know what kinds of personal information you collect. Anything you might gather and use for marketing or other purposes should be disclosed.

❑ ## EXPLAIN INFO USAGE

Let your visitors know exactly how the information you collect will or will not be used. If you sell or give away their data, disclose this. If not, provide assurances that you will never release any information to third parties.

❑ ## EXPLAIN PROTECTION PROTOCOLS

Provide details on how your visitor's information will be protected from hackers, scammers and nefarious usage. Give detailed specifications, linking to companies you use to ensure protection.

SITEMAPS

> Creating and submitting a Sitemap helps make sure that Google knows about all the pages on your site, including URLs that may not be discoverable by Google's normal crawling process.[27]
>
> –Google Search Console

WHAT THIS CHECKLIST IS ABOUT

There are two kinds of sitemaps: Those created for your site visitors and those created specifically for search engines. This checklist covers both, identifying key areas of how these sitemaps should be built, maintained and managed in order to ensure each provides you with the greatest impact on your web marketing.

WHY SITEMAPS ARE IMPORTANT

The goal of a sitemap is to help your visitors find the information they need quickly and efficiently. While both site navigation and internal site search options perform these functions as well, the importance of a well-designed sitemap cannot be understated. Whether you are building an HTML or XML sitemap, the goal is to deliver quality traffic to your internal site pages.

A well-crafted HTML sitemap can be crucial for helping visitors find your buried or hard-to-navigate-to pages. An XML sitemap, submitted to the search engines, can help ensure all relevant pages of your site are included in the search index, making them more likely to show up in the search results. Both types can play an important role in getting visitors to pages most relevant to their needs.

SITEMAP CHECKLIST

❑ ## KEEP IT CURRENT

Websites change. Pages are added, moved and/or deleted all the time. As these types of updates are made, your sitemaps must also be updated. Non-updated sitemaps run the risk of sending both visitors and search engines to the wrong pages, effectively destroying usability and corrupting your internal link flow.

❑ ## PRESENTED IN HIERARCHAL FORMAT

Your HTML sitemap should be more than a list of links to all your pages. Break the links up into sections corresponding to the hierarchal format of your main navigation. This allows visitors to find pages grouped together by topic, each group easily distinguishable from the next, so visitors get to the pages they need quickly.

❑ ## OPTIMIZE HTML SITEMAP

Your HTML sitemap may not be the first page you want visitors landing on coming from a search engine, nor should it be high on your list of pages to optimize for rankings. However, it's a good idea to spend a few minutes optimizing your sitemap for usability impact.

Here are a few things you can do to make your sitemap more robust and valuable for your visitors:

❑ ### INTRO PARAGRAPH

Open the sitemap with a quick intro paragraph. Position your sitemap to be a source of answers for the visitor's needs.

❑ ### INTRO TO MAIN SECTIONS

If your site is divided into sections, write a very brief intro to each section. Use keywords relevant to that section as a means to reinforce the content that follows.

❏ KEYWORD LINK TEXT & DESCRIPTIONS

Use keyword-rich text links followed by a short description of the page being linked to. Don't use page title tags as your link text; those are generally too long, or not written for this format. If possible, use your navigation link text (if optimized) as your sitemap links.

❏ PROPERLY LINKED IN SITE

Include a link to your sitemap in your global footer. This allows visitors to find any page on your site within two clicks, regardless of what page they are on. You should also add a link to your sitemap on your help and 404 pages.

❏ CREATE XML SITEMAP

It is often a good idea to create an XML sitemap specifically for search engines. Even though search engines can find your HTML sitemap, the XML format allows you to submit the sitemap page and track indexing of each page.

❏ LINK IN ROBOTS.TXT

Unlike an HTML sitemap, your XML sitemap isn't meant for visitors and is generally not something you want to link to from within the site. Link to the XML sitemap from your robots.txt file. Search engines will find it here and use it to begin spidering pages of your site.

Example
Sitemap: http://www.site.com/sitemap.xml

❏ SUBMIT TO SEARCH ENGINES

Use the search engine's sitemap submission tools to submit your sitemap for indexing. This allows you to get all your site pages in the search engine index for organic ranking assessment. However, if you have trouble getting pages indexed on their own, it might be a good idea to figure out why before creating or submitting the sitemap.

ON-PAGE OPTIMIZATION

Whenever I advise marketers on crafting pages, I ask them to put themselves in the minds of their potential visitors, and imagine a page that provides something so different and functional that it rises above everything else in its field.[28]

–Rand Fishkin
Moz

What This Checklist Is About

This checklist provides you with a reliable on-page optimization process designed to improve your site's search performance. While the term "SEO" covers a lot of ground, this on-page optimization checklist focuses on the optimization of a single web page. These tips, when applied to each landing page throughout your site (category, sub-category pages, etc.,) will help you create a more highly targeted and optimized website that will net you better search engine performance site-wide.

Why On-Page Optimization Is Important

There are three primary components of successful website optimization: Global site architecture; off-page marketing and promotion; and on-page, keyword-targeted optimization. Each plays a valuable role in the process of getting your site to perform strongly with search engines.

Fixing architecture issues generally eliminates destructive spider-stoppers. Off-page promotion is a great avenue for getting noticed. However, it's the on-page optimization that helps you focus your content on achieving top search engine placement for specific search queries. The first two have an effect on your rankings, but not as directly as on-page optimization.

As search engine algorithms evolve, on-page optimization has become a less significant piece of the web marketing puzzle. Yet it does maintain the most direct advantage over the other forms of online marketing, especially in terms of search engine rankings. While optimization rarely translates into top search engine rankings on its own, it is even rarer when rankings are achieved without any on-page optimization at all.

The optimization process is very checklist oriented. While other aspects of online marketing can lead you down many endless rabbit trails (albeit very important rabbit trails), on-page optimization has a beginning and an end for each page. It can be a good idea to regularly revisit and tweak optimized pages as needed, but once this checklist is complete, the significant work is done.

ON-PAGE OPTIMIZATION CHECKLIST

❏ CORE TERM RESEARCH

Before optimization of any page can begin, you first have to know what topics (or "core terms") are worth targeting. Start digging into keyword research tools to uncover relevant two- and even three-word phrases that represent a broad topic, specific to what you offer. Don't get bogged down worrying about the thousands of relevant long-tail keywords just yet. That comes later. The first step is to zero in on the topics that can be optimized on a page-by-page basis.

> **Examples**
> *motorcycle battery*
> *kids snow jackets*
> *industrial fire hose*

❏ KEY PHRASE RESEARCH

Further research into each core term can produce a list of hundreds, if not thousands, of additional phrases, each using the core term plus a relevant qualifier or other topically relevant phrases. Use your tools to uncover every possible phrase related to the core term.

Examples
honda motorcycle battery
kids spyder snow jackets
industrial fire hose nozzles

❏ ELIMINATE JUNK WORDS

Go through your list of phrases (core terms + qualifiers) and remove any that are too specific or are not relevant to what you offer. Look for words that just don't work for your business, such as "free," "cheap" or geo-targeted phrases that won't deliver the visitors you seek. Consider the intent of each keyword phrase, keeping only those that work for you and removing from your final list those that don't.

Examples
nebraska motorcycle battery
old motorcycle batteries
motorcycle battery art

❏ ORGANIZE YOUR PHRASES

Organize your final list of phrases into groups based on searcher intent. Most phrases can be categorized into categories for research, shopping, buying or learning. Each of these intents would require a different landing page with different content and calls to action. You can often group multiple phrases that fall under the same intent together. This allows you to optimize for more keywords without changing the focus of the page.

❏ GROUP SIMILAR PHRASES TOGETHER

If you still have a large number of keyword phrases in each "intent group," look for those that have similar meaning. Words such as "cheap" and "discount" can be used interchangeably, at least from the searcher's perspective, and a single page can be used to focus on these searchers.

You'll also find multiple variations of the same phrase such as plural, singular, active or past-tense versions. These will often work together on the same page as well. In the end, you should have one or more small groups of keywords, with each group corresponding to a single intent and purpose.

❏ SEARCH ENGINE ACCESSIBILITY

If the search engines have difficulty accessing certain pages of your site, then any on-page optimization you do for those pages will be pointless. Look at how you link to all your pages, making sure that none are too many clicks away from the home page. All navigation links need to be search engine spiderable, and the words you use in the links should be relevant and descriptive.

❏ USE STRUCTURED DATA

Incorporate schema.org structured data into your site's code. Search engines use this data to better understand key elements of your site, which translates into better interpretation for ranking value. It also impacts how these elements might display in search results. Review all relevant structured data for ecommerce, mobile, local, and general architecture.

❏ CANONICAL TAG USAGE

If your content management system allows the same content to be found via multiple URLs, choose one to be the canonical URL. Next implement a canonical tag on each of the other pages that lead to the same content. This provides a signal to the search engines letting them know which pages you want to receive all link and optimization value. It's still better to fix this kind of URL issue, but the canonical tag acts as a good band-aid.

Example

```
<link rel="canonical" href="http://www.site.com/
product/canonical-page.html" />
```

❏ REL="PREV"/"NEXT"

When you have a string of paginated pages, you want to make sure to use the rel tag to tell search engines which page comes before and which comes after in the chain. This is a valuable signal to the search engines that help them find/index all relevant content or products in the chain.

Example

```
<link rel="prev" href="https://www.polepositionmar-
keting.com/emp/" />
<link rel="next" href="https://www.polepositionmar-
keting.com/emp/page/3/" />
```

❑ OPTIMIZE URLS

URLs should follow a hierarchal structure similar to the navigation path used to get visitors to the page. Use keywords in both the directory and page names that are relevant to the content of the page. You also want to keep the URL as short as possible, using hyphens between words.

Examples
No: *www.site.com/pet-doors.html*
dog-door.html
www.site.com/cat-doors.html
Yes: *www.site.com/pet-doors/*
www.site.com/pet-doors/dog-doors/
www.site.com/pet-doors/dog-doors/large-dog-doors.html
www.site.com/pet-doors/dog-doors/small-dog-doors.html
www.site.com/pet-doors/cat-doors.html

❑ OPTIMIZE TITLE TAG

Your title tag is the single most important piece of optimizable real estate on each page, and you only have about seven words to work with. Be intentional about using your keywords, while also creating a compelling title tag that will entice visitors to click into your site from the search results. Keep in mind, search engines may change the clickable link from search results based on the keyword searched, so your optimized title tag may not always display.

Example
```
<title>Page Title Goes Here | Up to 65 Characters</title>
```

❑ BRAND TITLES

It can be helpful to add your business/brand name onto the end of your title tags. This can be a great way to build brand recognition in the minds of searchers during their research phase. Due to the limited space available, it is probably a good idea to truncate your brand name if/when needed to ensure your title tag conveys the best messaging possible. Also, place branding at the end, rather than the beginning of the title. Even if the title gets truncated in search results, the core message remains.

Examples

No: `<title>Replacement Motorcycle Batteries for All Makes and Models</title>`

No: `<title>BatteryStuff.com | Motorcycle Batteries for all Makes</title>`

Yes: `<title>Replacement Motorcycle Batteries for All Makes | BatteryStuff.com</title>`

❏ OPTIMIZE META DESCRIPTION

Your meta description is important only in as much as you need a compelling counterpart to your title tag when your page is displayed in the search results. Create a short, 160-character (or less) summary of what your visitors will find once they click the link to your page. Keywords are not as important as the call to action and benefits; however, just be sure the language of the meta description reinforces the specific content of the page.

Example
```
<meta name="description" content="Find a replacement
powersport battery for any make and model. Get powered
up for a start on every try. Fast, free shipping on
all motorcycle batteries.">
```

❏ IGNORE META KEYWORD TAG

Unless you are using the meta keyword tag for your internal site search, you can ignore it altogether. There is no search or usability advantage to optimizing this tag. Feel free to remove it completely.

❏ OPTIMIZE HEADING TAGS

Heading tags can be used both for search engine and visitor optimization. They make great scanning points to help readers quickly find the content they are most interested in, while also having a minor impact on your search ranking performance.

You don't need to add keywords into every heading on the page, but you definitely do want to keyword optimize your H1 tag, above the content. The longer the page's content, the more headings you'll want to incorporate to help break up the text into scannable chunks. Use keywords only when relevant.

Examples
```
<h1>High-Performance Motorcycle Battery Replacement</
    h1>
    <h2>Professionally Tested Motorsport Batteries</h2>
        <h3>The Perfect Start Every time</h3>
```

❏ HEADING TAG HIERARCHY

Heading tags range in hierarchy from H1 to H6. The H1 is the most important heading and each page should only have one, with few exceptions. Reserve the use of H2, H3 and H4 tags for content areas, while H5 and H6 heading tags can be used for developers to segment areas of the site, if necessary.

Examples
```
<h1>The Pages Most Important Headline, Usually at the
    Top</h1>
    <h2>Can Be Used as a Sub-Headline or for Second-
        Most Important Paragraph Headings</h3>
        <h3>Third-Most Important Heading for Breaking Up
            Content</h3>
```

❏ OPTIMIZE PAGE CONTENT

Your on-page content is the second most valuable area for optimization—behind title tags — both for visitors and search engines. Visible keywords let visitors know they found what they were looking for while giving search engines relevance for ranking the page. Use keywords to enhance each page's topic, but don't stuff them onto the page. Just write naturally, and keep the content topically focused and easy to read.

You also don't just want to focus on searched keywords, but also on related words and phrases that are typically associated with the topic. In fact, using related words can be an important aspect of optimizing content for the keywords you are targeting.

Example
No: *Our dog food is good food for your dog. Dogs love our dog food.*
Yes: *Our dog food is healthy, nutritious and gives your dog more energy.*

❑ MAKE TEXT SCANNABLE

Each page of your site should be easily scannable for those visitors who don't like to read every word on the page (which is most.) You can make content scannable by using bullet points, headings, bold text and short paragraphs. All of these can help the visitor quickly move through the content to find what they are most interested in reading, or what is most relevant to their needs.

❑ OPTIMIZE ALT ATTRIBUTE

You can create alternative (alt) text for each image of your site that is designed to display if the image doesn't load. This alt text can be lightly optimized for keywords, provided you maintain the intent of the attribute, which is to help visitors who cannot see the image understand its context.

Example

```
<img src="site.com/image.png" alt="Family Lawyer
Celebrates Victory After Winning Child Custody Case in
Cleveland OH.">
```

❑ OPTIMIZE LINK ANCHOR TEXT

Look for opportunities to use keywords as part of the link text when linking to specific pages of your site. Be sure not to spam your pages with a bunch of non-relevant links, or create links that all use the exact same anchor text. Be subtle and do what makes the most sense for each particular link.

Examples

No: *Click here to view our line of industrial fire hose products.*

No: *You'll find a complete line of industrial fire hoses.*
Check out these industrial fire hoses.
We have industrial fire hoses that can't be beat.
If you're looking for industrial fire hoses, look no further. How many times can I link industrial fire hoses before I get penalized?

Yes: *Check out our complete line of industrial fire hose products.*

❑ REVIEW PAGE FOR USABILITY

Above all else, each page of your site should focus most on the visitor's needs. Review and analyze each page, looking for visual and structural elements that can be improved to create a better user experience. Find things to keep the visitor more engaged with the content and moving through the conversion process to achieve the goals both you and they have.

❑ ADD CALLS TO ACTION

This point is mentioned in multiple other places throughout this book, and it's worth repeating due to its importance. Without a call to action, your content provides nowhere for your visitors to go or a path to follow next. Be sure to have at least one, if not a few, calls to action. Your primary call to action should be the most obvious.

LOCAL OPTIMIZATION

Forecasting SEO trends for local is quite difficult —
primarily because I know in my heart of hearts that
local SEO isn't a trend, phenomenon or fad. Local—
along with personalized search — is a necessary
evolution to truly optimize the search experience for
users across the globe.[29]

–Guillaume Bouchard
Search Engine Watch

WHAT THIS CHECKLIST IS ABOUT

Optimizing for local search results is similar to optimization in general. After all, good
optimization is always good optimization. However, getting listed in local search results
requires a bit more legwork. This checklist covers the essential elements of local optimization,
giving you the tasks needed to ensure search engines can correlate your site with the
all-important local signals.

WHY LOCAL OPTIMIZATION IS IMPORTANT

The single most performed activity on mobile browsers is search. That means people are
using their phones for finding things more than general web surfing.

The local search algorithm uses some very different signals to determine how businesses
rank. There are two primary signals used: One is the location of the searcher, and the
second is the location of the business. Based on these two factors, your business may get
very different placement in the search results.

While search engines may not default all searches from mobile devices to be "local," there are many that are inherently local, such as plumbers, lawyers or doctors, (just to name a few). But one of the key differences between local and organic search is that having a website is optional for local businesses. You can implement all of the external local signals and find yourself appearing in the local set of search results.

You can still get your website to rank organically for local-intent keyword phrases (i.e. "plumbers indianapolis"), but getting ranked in the local set provides additional advantages that the natural results don't offer. These benefits include showing your address, a map of your location and a click-to-call phone number all right there in the search results. This gives visitors the opportunity to bypass your site altogether and make an immediate connection with your business.

Failure to understand the importance of these signals, and carefully ensure that your business meets all of the criteria, can keep you from achieving top local search rankings. Keep in mind, the sites shown in the local set can be different for each searcher, but "optimizing" for local improves your chances of being in the local results more frequently and for more searchers.

LOCAL OPTIMIZATION CHECKLIST

❏ REVIEW NAP FOR CONSISTENCY

Make sure your name, address and phone number (NAP) are consistent throughout your site, as well as in local data aggregators. Search engines will cross-reference your information with providers such as InfoUSA, Acxiom, Factual and Localeze, to be sure they get the most accurate and reliable local information on your business as possible. Discrepancies between these signals can cause search engines and mapping software to provide incorrect data to searchers.

❏ USE STRUCTURED DATA

Be sure to incorporate structured data (schema.org) into your website's coding around elements that are specific to location-based data. Structured data can help search engines easily identify your NAP and other local signals.

❑ SUBMIT TO LOCAL DIRECTORIES

Submit your site to local aggregators. These citations help improve your local relevance for searches performed within your geographical area. Use services such as SuperPages, CitySearch, InsiderPages and YellowPages.com, as well as any other sources that are specific for your location or industry.

In addition, find industry and niche directories that you can be listed in. Build relationships with other authoritative sites, such as your local chamber of commerce, Better Business Bureau, etc. Optimize all your listings with images, and local and keyword category tags. Write descriptions that act as a call to action to visit your site.

❑ GET REVIEWED

Encourage customers to write reviews of your business, products or services and publish them on sites such as Google+, CitySearch and Yelp. Don't be afraid of asking for reviews in emails, physical signage, on invoices, etc. Make submitting reviews easy by providing links whenever possible. Be careful not to offer anything in return for a review, as that can be seen as review-buying, which is a violation of many terms of services.

You want your reviews to be natural and happen regularly rather than several at a time. Once a review is complete, it may be okay to provide a small reward such as a discount or a gift card; however, this should not be disclosed ahead of time. You will want to verify the terms of each review site to ensure you stay within their guidelines.

❑ GOOGLE MY BUSINESS

Google helps local businesses manage their business information and reviews, and it lets you interact with customers. It is especially important for establishing your local credentials for locality based searches. This is a powerful tool that is an important part of local optimization.

❑ LINK TO REVIEW SITES

It can be a good idea to create a feedback page on your website that links to your review profiles. This creates a non-invasive way of soliciting a review that customers can utilize at their leisure. Just like adding social sharing buttons, you are simply creating the opportunity, then letting your visitors decide whether to follow through or not.

LANDING PAGES

> Landing page optimization is no longer a well-kept secret. It has rapidly become the most powerful method that smart Internet marketers use to build a lasting competitive advantage. Well-optimized landing pages and websites can change the economics of your business overnight and turbocharge your online marketing programs.[30]
>
> –Tim Ash, Maura Ginty, Rich Page
> *Landing Page Optimization*

What This Checklist Is About

Landing pages aren't just for PPC. In fact, a page that has been properly optimized for search can also work as a good landing page for your pay-per-click and other paid ad campaigns. This checklist helps you create great optimized landing pages for both SEO and PPC strategies.

Why Landing Pages Are Important

We all know that search engines look at the quality of a page as part of determining its relevance for a particular search. While search engines might use different algorithms for determining relevance for paid and organic results, the idea behind page quality is the same. The higher relevance a page has to the topic, the higher placement it will achieve.

We often think of PPC landing pages and optimized pages as being two separate pages altogether. But in many cases they can be one in the same. Landing pages need to be optimized, and optimized pages need to act as effective landing pages. The goal for both is the same: Get the sale!

Creating an optimized landing page is about creating a page that works great for both PPC and SEO purposes. If your organically optimized page isn't a good landing page for conversions, then you're throwing away good money. You want just as good of a conversion rate for your organic traffic as you get for your paid traffic.

There are some cases where it makes better sense to deliver PPC traffic to a non-optimized page—one designed specifically for paid traffic. However for most situations, you should be able to drop your paid traffic onto your optimized pages and see a strong result. The key is to make sure that you don't drop them on a page that has only been optimized for rankings, but one that has been optimized for conversions, too.

LANDING PAGE CHECKLIST

❏ COMPELLING, KEYWORD-FOCUSED TITLE TAG

The title tag is a significant part of creating an effective optimized landing page. It's probably the most important five to eight words you'll write. Your page titles need to not only utilize your keywords, they must also be compelling enough for the searcher to choose your link over the 10-plus others on the first page. Anybody can throw keywords into a title tag, but it takes craftsmanship to create a title that will both get ranked and get more clicks than your competitors.

Example
```
<title>10 Ways to Take Your Business from Bust to
Boom!</title>
```

❏ COMPELLING META DESCRIPTION TAG

While the meta description has little significance for ranking purposes, it is still a key component for optimization. This description displays in the search results and can be a key factor in enticing potential visitors to click into your site. Use this space to create a strong call to action for the searcher. The goal is to be more compelling than the other descriptions above and below you in the search results.

Example

```
<meta name="description" content="Running a successful
business isn't easy. If your business could use a
boost, try these 10 strategies that will propel you
into even greater profits."/>
```

❏ ATTENTION-GETTING HEADLINE

The headline at the top is one of the very first things visitors see once they hit your landing page. As such, you want to maintain the "scent" from the search query to the title used in the search results, and then to the page itself. Using keywords here is critical for this consistency.

The headline should be placed in an H1 tag for proper optimization. Don't use this space merely to state a closed fact. Create a compelling headline that gives visitors a reason to continue engaging with the page.

Examples
No: *How to Gain New Business in Just 10 Weeks*
Yes: *10 Tips in 10 Weeks = 1000s of New Customers in Under Three Months*!

❏ BENEFIT-FOCUSED CONTENT

The content of your optimized landing page must maintain its focus on the topic and on the goals to be achieved. Long-winded or meandering content will cause your visitors to lose interest before they even get to the call to action. Be sure you address your visitor's needs by providing the benefits they receive when they take the action noted. Like the page headline, the content should also maintain a keyword scent throughout.

❏ USE PROPER CONTENT HIERARCHY

Use as many words as necessary to achieve your goals, ensuring long content is easily skimmable. Not everything you write will be essential to every visitor. Use paragraph headings and sub-headings to give visitors a way to move quickly to information that is important to them. Proper content hierarchy helps visitors skim and scan the page while keeping them engaged until they have enough information to make a decision for their next course of action.

❏ VISUAL CLARITY

Cluttered pages create distracted visitors, and distracted visitors don't complete the goals you want. Keep your pages visually clean and appealing with as few distractions as possible. White space helps, and adjusting things as simple as line height, paragraph spacing and image margins can contribute to the overall readability of the content. Keep it nice, clean and tidy.

❏ SECURE INBOUND LINKS

Quality inbound links give the search engines an understanding of a page's topical relevance before they even have a chance to analyze the page itself. In the most basic of terms, links create a signal as to how popular a page is. Establishing quality links pointing to your landing pages can help increase each page's search performance, while driving additional relevant traffic to your site.

❏ INCLUDE SOCIAL SHARING OPTIONS

Social signals are growing in importance in search engine algorithms. Therefore, it's important that your optimized landing pages can easily be shared to your visitors' social networks.

Social sharing buttons allow your visitors to spread the word and drive traffic for you—doing almost all the heavy lifting themselves. For free. Because they want to! The more your visitors engage with your content, the more likely they are to accomplish the goals you desire, come back for more and bring others with them to do the same.

❏ CLEAR CALL TO ACTION

Without a call to action, the landing page is useless. Each page has to have a goal and desired action (or set of actions) that you want visitors to take. Lacking a strong call to action on the page, visitors may leave, never having received an appealing reason to take the next step. The only way to get the visitors to the goal is to tell them what the goal is and how they achieve it.

❏ TEST CHANGES

Very rarely does a one-time pass get a page to rank in the number one spot, or achieve the highest conversion rate possible. Testing and tweaking each of the areas above will allow you to continue to improve the page incrementally. A good landing page is always under construction. Test for rankings, test for conversions, and keep testing. The more you test, the more you'll be able increase both the traffic and sales your landing page delivers.

IMAGE OPTIMIZATION

> If you run an online store, image optimization is an
> art that you want to master. From attracting shoppers
> perusing Google images to reducing site load time—
> image optimization can be an important part of
> building a successful ecommerce business.[31]
>
> –Mark Hayes
> Shopify

WHAT THIS CHECKLIST IS ABOUT

This list covers several aspects of image optimization that affect both how images are displayed on the website, and how they are found in search and social spheres. Optimizing images can improve your site's performance by helping visitors find items and information they want faster. How your images are presented to the searcher as they search or engage online can also help—or hurt—your website.

WHY IMAGE OPTIMIZATION IS IMPORTANT

Many businesses still don't understand the value of image search. While most B2B businesses won't necessarily benefit directly from having images found in search results, many B2C and ecommerce businesses do. While basic image searches have been performed on Google for years, image-based social sites such as Pinterest are showing exponential growth in popularity as people search by image rather than by keyword query.

Properly optimizing your images can serve several purposes. One is to ensure your images are being downloaded and displayed properly on your site and that they are not causing speed issues for your visitors. This plays a role for both visitor usability, and search engine indexing and ranking. Another purpose is to have your images displayed in the search results pages, either in the natural results or in a specific image search.

For many searchers, looking through images can help them find products faster. Instead of spending hours navigating through dozens of sites hoping the site has what they want, an image search allows visitors to scan through hundreds of products across many more websites in only a few minutes. These images get them to the products they want faster with less time spent searching.

When your images show up in the search results or on social media sites, you're opening up a new avenue of potential traffic. While not all of this traffic will be ready to buy, you do have the opportunity to reach a prequalified visitor. When someone finds you with a general search, they are still hoping you have what they want. With image search, they already know and liked it enough to click through!

IMAGE OPTIMIZATION CHECKLIST

❑ READABLE FILE NAME

Use readable file names for all your images. Avoid using numbers or characters that have little or no meaning to anyone but you. Instead, use relevant words that describe what the image is. In fact, feel free to use keywords relevant to each image. Also, be sure to use a hyphen between words rather than spaces.

Example
No: *www.site.com/bvs294835.png*
No: *www.site.com/batman vs superman.png*
Yes: *www.site.com/batman-vs-superman.png*

❑ INCLUDE ALT ATTRIBUTE

All images should include an alt attribute. Write alt text that describes the visuals of the image and can act as a supplement if the image doesn't display. If you feel the image provides only visual value, the alt attribute can be left blank. However, it's a good idea to use it anyway just for reference.

Example
```
<img src="site.com/image.png" alt="man sitting on
crescent of moon"/>
```

❏ ADD IMAGE TITLE

The image title can be used to provide a pop-up "tool-tip" in the browser. This is a great place to add additional information that you would like visitors to see when they mouse-over the image. An image's title and alt text should both be unique.

Example

```
<img src="site.com/image.png" title="Man on the
Moon"/>
```

❏ NO KEYWORD STUFFING

Don't stuff keywords into your image alt or title tags for "SEO" purposes. These tags should be used for descriptive purposes only. Adding keywords to each is acceptable, provided they are used within proper context and doing so provides value to the visitor. If the keywords you want to add are not appropriate for the image, don't do it.

Examples

No: *Our dog food is good dog food for your dog. Dogs love our dog food.*

Yes: *Our dog food is healthy, nutritious and gives your dog more energy.*

❏ PROPER IMAGE FORMAT

There are three primary image formats for the web: .jpg, .png and .gif. Each offers unique properties and is better for certain types of images over others. Choose the format for each image that produces the highest quality in the smallest size possible.

❏ REDUCE IMAGE SIZE

Reduce each image's file size as much as possible, without sacrificing the integrity of the image's clarity. Image size reduction can be accomplished by selecting the right format, size and the proper resolution when the image is created. There are also tools that will "optimize" images after they have been created as well. Use these tools to keep your images fast-loading while maintaining superb quality.

❏ ADD IMAGE CAPTIONS

Image captions are some of the most-read text on a page. Adding captions to display below key images can help reinforce critical concepts you want to be sure your visitors know. Write quality, keyword-optimized text for image captions wherever needed, to reinforce the message of each page.

❏ NO TEXT IN IMAGES

Don't put valuable text in image format. Instead, make sure important text is always in HTML so search engine spiders can read it, and it will be included as part of the page's content analysis. Only content without any true value to your visitors (or is already repeated in the main text) should be included as part of an image.

❏ MULTIPLE IMAGE SIZES

You never know what size screen your images will be viewed on. In order to ensure the image viewed is in the highest possible quality, while also being as small (in byte size) as possible, create multiple images in various sizes. Use proper programming to make sure the most appropriately sized image will display based on the screen resolution.

❏ USE CSS SPRITES

The more images on a web page, the longer the page takes to download, even when the images are relatively small. When a page uses multiple images, use image sprites to combine them all into a single, faster-loading image. Then use CSS to display only the portion of that larger image that is relevant to that particular place on the page. This will reduce the number of server calls, resulting in faster page download times.

❏ SPIDERABLE IMAGES

Make sure your images are spiderable by the search engines. Don't block them in your robots.txt file and always use true HTML to link to each image. Images linked with JavaScript may not be easily indexed by search engines, if at all.

❏ **CREATE IMAGE XML SITEMAP**

If you really want to get your images indexed by the search engines, create an XML sitemap specifically for images. Submit that sitemap to Webmaster Tools to ensure the search engines can find them all.

❏ **DON'T REMOVE OLD (PRODUCT) IMAGES**

Old images, even for discontinued products, can still be a source of relevant traffic. Don't remove those images. Instead, when the image is clicked, bring the user to the most relevant page currently existing on your site. Be careful that the page you lead them too isn't too far removed from what they were expecting when they clicked the image link.

❏ **ADD IMAGE SOCIAL SHARING ICONS**

Add social sharing options that allow your visitors to post your images to their social networks. Give visitors the option to tweet, pin or otherwise share the image, ensuring the credit (link value and otherwise) leads back to you.

PDF OPTIMIZATION

PDF is great for one thing and one thing only: printing documents. Paper is superior to computer screens in many ways, and users often prefer to print documents that are too long to easily read online.[32]

–Jakob Nielsen
Nielsen Norman Group

WHAT THIS CHECKLIST IS ABOUT

PDFs should never be used as a replacement for a traditional web page; however, some types of content are best delivered in PDF format. This checklist covers a handful of PDF optimization tasks that will help you ensure your PDFs achieve maximum potential on the web.

WHY PDF OPTIMIZATION IS IMPORTANT

In most instances, a standard web page will give you the flexibility that you need without disrupting the visitor's onsite experience. But even when your web pages are able to be printed in an appealing format, you still don't have the type of control that a PDF offers. That may not matter for 90% of your online content, but for the other 10%, it really matters.

There are many reasons why the PDF format may be the best option for a particular piece of content. Usually, it's preferable for longer-form content that is better read more as a book than as a long web page. But the value of PDFs is that they give you precise control over how your information is presented.

Unfortunately, many people forget about optimizing their PDFs for both search and for readers. Just as with traditional web pages, if you want your PDF content to be found and consumed, it must be optimized.

Many of the PDF optimization principles are the same as with traditional web pages, but the processes are different. Which is why it's especially important to optimize properly. Remember, you're not just optimizing for search (keyword optimization for better exposure and clicks). You're optimizing for people as well (compression and file reduction for faster downloads). Optimizing your PDFs creates a nearly seamless web experience for any visitor who comes across these valuable documents.

PDF OPTIMIZATION CHECKLIST

❑ USE TEXT-BASED FILES

Just like a web page, if you want to get your PDFs indexed, you need to make sure they are text rather than image based. Images are great and can be used in your PDF documents for visual flair or illustrations, but the bulk of the document needs to be plain text.

❑ SEARCH-FRIENDLY FILE NAME

The PDF file name is akin to the URL of a web page. As with web page URLs, make sure the file name is keyword relevant and search friendly. In most cases, the file name will become part of the URL used to access the document.

> **Examples**
> Word Document Filename:
> > *Best Damn Web Marketing Checklist Period.docx*
> Saved PDF Filename:
> > *best-damn-web-marketing-checklist-period.pdf.*

❑ OPTIMIZE CONTENT

Just like any other optimized web page, you want to optimize your PDF content for the keyword topics you want to rank for. In fact, follow all the standard content optimization procedures found in this book.

❏ ADD ALT TEXT TO IMAGE

Add alt text to your PDF images just like a web page. Well, not just like that, because the process is different, but the value is the same. Be succinct, but descriptive, using any relevant keywords.

❏ SET READING LANGUAGE

You can also set the PDF reading language. Search engines use language settings in web pages to inform them on language issues. It's likely they will do the same with your PDFs.

❏ OPTIMIZE TITLE PROPERTY

The PDF title property is akin to the title tag of a web page. This will be what search engines show as the clickable link when the PDF appears in the search results. As with any title, you want to optimize this for keywords and generating clicks.

❏ OPTIMIZE SUBJECT

The PDF subject is similar to the meta description of a web page. Search engines may or may not choose to use it. However, if they do, you want to make sure it adds value and generates clicks.

❏ LINK BACK TO YOUR WEBSITE

Many PDFs are viewed in a web browser like traditional web pages, or on tablets. Add links back to your website as appropriate to make it easy for readers to find your site (again). Be sure to use relevant anchor text so, once your PDF is indexed, the links will count like standard web page links. Note: If your PDF is primarily for offline viewing, provide the full URL rather than or in addition to a text link. This will at least give printed-page readers a way to visit the reference if they are inclined to type the full URL into their browser later.

❏ USE STANDARD FONTS

Only six fonts are supported by all PDF readers: Times, Helvetica, Courier, Symbol, and Zapf Dingbats. Any other fonts used must be embedded into the PDF, which increases the PDF file size. If you don't embed non-supported fonts, Adobe will automatically substitute one of the standard fonts. This, of course, causes you to lose control over the visual layout, which is one of the main benefits of using the PDF format to begin with.

❏ FEWER FONTS

Every font used in your document adds additional kilobytes to your PDF file size. The fewer number of fonts used, the smaller your PDF data size can be.

❏ LIMIT FONT STYLES

Not only does using more fonts increase the size, but every font style is treated as a different font. Every time you italicize, bold or bold-italicize words, you're increasing font usage. This becomes especially important when using non-standard fonts that have to be embedded. Each style variation is a new font embed.

❏ USE VECTOR-BASED IMAGES

When available, use vector-based image files. These images are smaller and of higher quality than bitmap images.

❏ USE MONOCHROME BITMAP IMAGES

If you can't use vector-based images and are using bitmaps instead, make them monochrome rather than color. This will keep bitmap images as small as possible.

❏ SAVE AS MINIMUM SIZE

When saving a Word document to PDF format, look for the option to "save as minimum size." This saves the PDF specifically for web use.

❏ ENABLE FAST WEB VIEW

Fast web view restructures the PDF so pages can be downloaded one at a time rather than forcing the entire document to be downloaded at once. This is especially important for large PDF documents that are likely to be viewed in the browser.

❏ ESTABLISH INITIAL VIEW SETTINGS

Adobe gives you options to set how you want the PDF to be seen upon being opened. Here you can set whether or not the navigation tab is open by default, the visible page layout, window size, and other options. Determine how you want the PDF to be viewed and establish the settings accordingly.

❏ CHECK COMPATIBILITY

Avoid saving your PDF in the most recent version of Adobe Acrobat. Go a couple of versions lower than the latest to ensure most readers or search engines won't have issues viewing the document.

❏ LINK TO YOUR PUBLISHED PDF

Search engines find documents and pages via links in other web pages. Be sure to strategically link to your PDF just as you would any other page to ensure it gets found by search engines.

BLOGGING

> Informed and educated visitors become confident, loyal customers…. Too many marketers focus on gaining initial visibility through advertising or attention-seeking stunts…. With a blog you can hold prospects' interest for longer, winning customers round over time, and bringing them back to hear from you long after their first contact.[33]
>
> –Chris Garrett
> Wordtracker

What This Checklist Is About

Blogging is as easy as choosing a blogging platform and writing regularly, just as racing is as easy as starting a car and pushing on the gas pedal. Anyone can blog, but blogging effectively takes planning, strategizing and careful crafting of your message. This list covers blog set-up, important functionality, writing your posts and publishing. These tips will help you go from rookie to pro blogger in 6.5 posts (or something like that).

Why Blogging Is Important

Your blog is (or should be) the center-point of all your social efforts. Everything you do in the social sphere should ultimately lead back to your blog. While engagement on other social channels allows you to broadcast your message within set confines and parameters, your blog is the only place where you have 100% control of the message. You can publish in any format, and the only restrictions are those you choose to set for yourself.

Face it: You don't own your Twitter stream. You don't own your LinkedIn profile. You don't own your Facebook page. At any moment, those services can hide your stream, censor your messaging, suspend your profile or fall into relative obscurity. (Remember MySpace?) While they make great broadcast and interaction platforms, under the right (or wrong) circumstances, you can lose everything in a matter of minutes.

This means you need a place where you control the message. Where you get to say what you want to say without having to limit your characters, worry about your choice of words (though self-censorship is always appreciated) or be fearful of losing years of critical content because yet another social network gets abandoned by the masses. That place is your blog.

In all your tweeting, sharing and engaging on social networks, the goal is to bring people to your website. Since you don't want to annoy your audience with the persistent hard-selling of your main site pages, that leaves your blog as the primary place to drive social traffic. Your blog is the area of the site where visitors can learn more about the things you're passionate about. Where they come to get new tips and tricks. Where they read educational content they find valuable. Where you are, ultimately, soft-selling them on your brand, products and services.

If you do a good job blogging, a good chunk of your audience will realize they need what you offer. The more valuable your blog, the more likely you are to turn social visitors into paying customers.

BLOGGING CHECKLIST

❏ KNOW YOUR PURPOSE

Before you start blogging, you need to know what you're doing it for. Why do you want or need a blog? Your answer shouldn't be, "Because I read it in a checklist." Rather, it should have something to do with achieving your business goals. Your business blog must have a business-oriented purpose. What's yours?

❏ BUILD PERSONAS

The target audience for your blog might be different than your main website. On your site, you're looking strictly for customers. On your blog, your audience might be your competition, industry experts, potential customers or people who influence your industry. Build personas to better understand who your target audience is so you can write content specifically for them. Maybe they are do-it-yourselfers, educators, trainers, trainees, or any number of other things. Regardless, you need to know how best to create content that meets their needs.

❏ LISTEN TO YOUR AUDIENCE

Spend some time just listening to your audience. What are they saying on Twitter, Facebook and LinkedIn? What type of blog posts are they writing? What comments are they making on other platforms? As you listen, look for unmet needs, unanswered questions and information not being provided by other bloggers or sources. Document what you find in a text document or spreadsheet as this will become the basis of your messaging going forward.

❏ DETERMINE YOUR MESSAGE

You have to decide what kind of blog you want to have. Will you focus on education, sales or industry information? Will you provide solutions or show your audience how to get solutions for themselves? Determine your primary message type and focus on that. It is okay to have a main focus and multiple sub-focuses, but don't let anything overshadow your primary message.

❏ SELECT YOUR GOALS

Every blog needs goals. Without goals, you have no way to determine if your efforts are successful or not. Sit down and write them out, making sure they are realistic, attainable and worthwhile. Set reachable benchmarks to hit along the way so you can monitor progress daily, weekly, monthly or yearly.

❏ CHOOSE A PLATFORM

Choosing a blogging platform is no small matter. It's the equivalent of laying the foundation for a building. The wrong foundation can crumble underneath you, no matter how beautiful of a structure you have on top of it. Research the pros and cons of each platform and determine what will best serve your business needs.

❏ BUILT ON YOUR DOMAIN

If you want to control your message, then you have to host the blog yourself. Regardless of what blogging platform you choose, your blog should, without exception, be hosted on your own domain. Assuming you already have an established business URL, be sure to place your blog in a sub-folder, not a sub-domain, as this gives you the best search engine marketing benefit.

Examples
No: *www.bloghost.com/blog*
No: *blog.yoursite.com*
Yes: *www.yoursite.com/blog*

❏ SET 'WWW.'

If you are setting up your blog on an existing site, you likely already have this established (see Domain Name & URLs checklist), but it's a good idea to double check. Decide if you are going to use the "www." in your blog URLs or not. Find the option in your blog settings to choose the one you want. This ensures that all your URLs will be uniform, either with or without the www.

Examples
Either: *yoursite.com/blog*
Or: *www.yoursite.com/blog*

❏ CUSTOMIZE URLS

Most blogging platforms allow you to customize your URLs so they can be more keyword and search engine friendly. The best URLs are those that use part of the post title, truncated for simplicity and keyword relevance. Avoid URLs that would be difficult to type out in the browser URL bar.

Examples
No: *yoursite.com/blog /category/an-example-of-a-very-long-blog-*
     post-title-that-translates-into-a-very-long-url/3456434
Yes: *yoursite.com/blog /category/long-url-shortened*

❏ PROVIDE SUBSCRIPTION OPTIONS

You want to create a way for your readers to subscribe to your blog feed. This allows them to be notified when new posts are published so they can come back to read them at their leisure.

❏ RSS FEED

An RSS newsfeed is a great way for your blog readers to be notified when you've published a new post. As much as you want to generate traffic to your site, it's better to let visitors see when you have posted updates without having to visit your blog and remember what they read last.

❏ TWITTER FEED

Twitter is a great place to post links to newly published posts. You should have a Twitter feed, anyway, but if you have an especially active blog, it may be worthwhile to create a feed that is used solely for pushing out your posts.

❏ EMAIL SUBSCRIPTION

Give visitors the option to subscribe to your blog by way of a daily or weekly email that lets them know what posts are new. This allows them to get a nice roundup of new posts and skim through to see what they are interested in reading.

❏ CHOOSE FULL TEXT OR SUMMARY RSS FEED

Decide if you want your blog's RSS feed subscribers to see the full post in their reader or just a summary. Full text feeds allow them to read the complete post directly from their readers without ever visiting your site. Summary feeds show only a small portion of each post, requiring visitors to click to your site to read the rest. Summary feeds generate more traffic to your site, but also reduce the number of people who will actually read the full post. You have to decide which is better for your business goals.

❏ OPEN TO SEARCH ENGINES

Be sure your blog is accessible to search engines so they can index your posts and include them in the search results. When a blog is in development, search engine access is usually shut off, for good reason. Don't forget to flip the switch when your blog goes live. Search engines are a great source of traffic. Don't shut them out.

❏ SEARCH FUNCTION

Make sure your blog has a search function that allows visitors to find content they are interested in. Most readers won't scroll through post after post looking for content, but they'll perform a quick search on your blog to see if you have a post about whatever they're looking for.

❏ CUSTOMIZABLE TITLE TAGS

You want to be able to write a customized title tag for each post. Most blogging platforms use the post title as the title tag by default. While this seems to make sense, post titles don't always make the best titles for display in the search results. By customizing your title tags, you control the length and the keywords that search engines analyze and searchers see, without having to change the actual titles of your blog posts.

❏ CUSTOMIZABLE META DESCRIPTION TAGS

As with your title tags, you also want to be able to customize your meta description tags on each post. Again, this allows you to control the message that is most likely to be displayed in the search results. By default, most search engines and social platforms use the first few sentences of the blog post or information placed in a summary field, neither of which is sure to make a compelling meta description.

❏ ALLOW COMMENTS

Will you allow readers to comment on your posts? There are very few situations where this is a bad idea. In fact, posts that don't allow comments, by nature, have less engagement than those that do. If you are trying to establish relationships with your readers, comments are a great way to begin that interaction. Don't expect every comment to be positive. Give people room to disagree with you.

I should note that there is a growing trend to turn off comments completely in favor of using social media for all engagement. This has its merits but also its drawbacks. Consider which is best for you. If you allow comments, it is probably a good idea to only keep them open for a short period of time. Once the post is 2-4 weeks old, the only comments it's likely to receive will be spam.

❏ BLOCK SPAM

To keep your comments under control, you'll want to implement some kind of spam blocker. While it may not be an issue in the early days of blogging, without some kind of spam control in place, you'll find yourself sorting through dozens, if not hundreds, of spam comments. Even the best spam blockers still let some spam through, so pay attention to the incoming comments and only allow those that you know to be genuine.

❏ COMMENT SUBSCRIPTION

Allow visitors to subscribe to the comments on each post. Most comment subscription tools email the visitor anytime a new comment is posted to a blog post they are subscribed to. This allows them to stay engaged with the conversation and come back to contribute additional thoughts, or reply to a comment someone else made after their own.

❏ BACKUP REGULARLY

Perform regular backups of your database so you can restore all your data if something really bad happens. Platforms such as WordPress have plugins that will manage regular backups for you; however, I always like to have a backup backup plan. Contact your web host to make sure they back up your site and databases regularly as well.

❏ CUSTOM CONTENT CONCLUSION

Some platforms and plugins will allow you to create a separate message to append to the end of each blog post. This is a great place to put sales messages about your products or services, or highlight other information you think your readers will want to know. It's a good idea to switch up this information regularly so your readers don't become too accustomed to any one message—and ignore all of them.

❏ CATEGORIZE POSTS

Create a list of blog categories that will be the core topic of the posts you will cover. Keep this list succinct (7-10 categories max). All posts should be able to fit into one of these categories. If not, the post probably isn't right for your blog.

❏ OFFER RELATED POSTS

At the end of each post, it can also be a good idea to offer links to additional content the visitor might be interested in reading. This content should be somewhat related to what they just read, offering links to other posts on the same, or similar, topic for their further education.

❏ CHECK FOR BROKEN LINKS

You should regularly check your blog for broken links. If you are linking out to other sources, over time those sources disappear or are moved to different URLs. A regular broken link check will allow you to keep old blog posts current, ensuring every link continues to point to a proper URL.

❏ INSTALL ANALYTICS

Be sure to install analytics tracking code in your blog so you can analyze how your audience interacts with your content. If one blog post is particularly popular, this can give you ideas for similar blog posts. Analytics tracking is also necessary for you to track your blog's business goals.

❏ SET UP SOCIAL SHARING

Make it easy for your visitors to share your blog posts with their followers. Install social sharing options that appear either at the top, bottom or side of each blog post. This allows your visitors to share any post with a simple click of a button. The best way to broadcast your writing brilliance is to let someone else do it for you!

❏ ESTABLISH AUTHOR GUIDELINES

Whether you're a solo blogger or have multiple authors on your blog, create guidelines so you can maintain a certain element of consistency. It's okay for each author to have their own voice, but author guidelines help ensure you keep your brand messaging clear between them all.

Here are some guidelines that you might want to establish for your authors:

❏ TOPICS TO COVER

You might assign topics for each of your authors to cover, or you can give all authors full breadth within a range of industry topics you want to focus on. It's also a good idea to list specific topics you may want to avoid.

❏ POST TITLES

The post title is the most important part of the post. Set guidelines on what titles should achieve and how you want them written.

❏ LENGTH OF POSTS

Longer posts get good traction, if the quality is good, but not every post needs to be *War and Peace*. It's a good idea to mix up post length, but be sure to set some guidelines so things don't get out of hand. Whatever length range you set, allow for some exceptions when warranted.

❏ FORMATTING

Set guidelines on how posts are to be formatted. Decide how you will use headings, bullets, emphasis and bolding, and whether or not those will be required for each post.

❏ LANGUAGE & TONE

Let your authors know what kinds of words they are not permitted to use. Some blogs are extremely liberal in their language, and that works for them. Others might want to have no-swearing or no-criticism policies in place.

❏ VOICE

Decide on a primary voice for your blog. While each author can have their own distinctive dialect of that voice, you want to maintain a level of consistency in how the posts are written. Decide if you're going to have a professional, humorous, snarky, etc., voice and ensure all authors follow that format.

❏ IMAGE USAGE

Determine how images are to be used in each post. This includes image source, sourcing, size, captions and placement. You also want to set guidelines about image licensing and attribution. No sense setting yourself up for a lawsuit by using an unauthorized image!

❏ LINKING

Determine what policies you will establish for linking to external content and/or self-promotional sources. Links aren't bad, but there should be some constraints to avoid abuse.

❏ QUOTING

Quoting other works is always a great exercise. Set guidelines on how quoting will be done, and to what extent. For the most part, you can't do it too much, provided it doesn't slip into the realm of what would be considered stealing someone else's content. Also be sure to establish guidelines for proper attribution of quoted content.

❏ PROOFING AND APPROVAL PROCESSES

If you want each post approved before being published, establish guidelines for submitting posts for approval and for another level of proofreading. Determine how far in advance posts must be submitted and the process it goes through once it is.

❏ BIO

Each blogger's bio should be relatively uniform. Determine what you will or won't allow in the author's bio and what must be included.

❏ COMMENT RESPONSES

If you get negative comments, it might be a good idea to have policies in place as to how your company will respond to those comments. Generally, you want to respond positively with a helpful attitude. While that sounds obvious, without such policies in place you might be surprised by what you get!

❑ **GUESTS POSTS**

Determine whether or not guest posts will be accepted. If so, all guest post authors must adhere to the same requirements and guidelines as the regular authors. It's also probably a good idea to post your guidelines for guest posts to keep the submission spam down to a minimum.

❑ **SAVE IDEAS**

Anytime you or members of your team have an idea for a blog post, write it down and store it somewhere. Great ideas often come at the most awkward times, usually when we have no chance of following through on them immediately. Having a place to store ideas allows you to go back to a nice well of thoughts and possibilities when the idea pool has otherwise run dry.

❑ **CREATE AN EDITORIAL CALENDAR**

Whether it's just you, or you're managing an entire blogging team, you should create an editorial calendar to keep your posting on track. Blogging can often be easily shoved aside for "more important" matters, especially when there is no due date for your next post. A publishing calendar helps spread out the blogging duties, ensures you have a stream of topics to write about, and prevents your blog from dying from inadvertent neglect.

An editorial calendar can also help you focus on creating a variety of content and visuals. It's easy to write posts, but creating visuals, infographics, audio and/or video content all take additional time. Use your editorial calendar to plan and help you execute these additional forms of content.

❑ **WRITE A KILLER POST TITLE**

When someone reads the title of a post in their RSS reader or their social streams, you've got one chance to compel them to click through to read it. That means your post title must be absolutely awesome. Since the title often sets the tone for the post, even great post content will seem less interesting with an uninteresting title.

Examples
No: *SEO Mistakes People Often Make*
Yes: *How to Avoid an SEO Disaster of Monumental Proportions*
No: *How to Create a Landing Page*
Yes: *Why My Landing Page Beats Your SEO and PPC Landing Pages Every Time!*

❏ STIMULATING INTRO

You grabbed their attention with the title. Now, you need to continue to sell it with the first few sentences of your post. Your first paragraph must be interesting, stimulating and engaging so your readers are compelled to keep reading the rest of it. If you don't grab them in the first few sentences, you'll be lucky if they even scan the rest of the post.

❏ COMPELLING CONTENT

Keep your full post exciting, entertaining and informational. Don't just write for the sake of writing, but make sure you write something worthy of being read and shared. If you can't do that, then maybe you need to write a different post!

❏ APPEALING IMAGES

Each post should be accompanied by an appealing image. An image is a visual way of conveying the content of the post at a single glance. A good image draws the visitor in to read the post. While each post should always have at least one image at or near the top, using multiple images throughout is a great way to keep the reader visually engaged all the way through. Consider using animated gifs, infographics, quoted text and screenshots throughout your post. If your audience is active on visual social networks, such as Pinterest, consider a text overlay on the first image of your post with the post title.

❏ SKIMMABLE

Keep your blog post content both skimmable and scannable to the eye. Many readers don't want to read every word, but they will scan the post for quick takeaways. Using multiple headings, images and bulleted (or numbered) lists in your posts helps break up long, chunks of content. If readers see something that interests them, they are then more likely to stop and read.

❏ ASK QUESTIONS

One way to engage readers is to ask questions. This gets them thinking about the answers and is helpful in encouraging them to comment on your posts, or write an answer to it on their own blog or social networks. Use questions to get your audience thinking about things in a new way, which is another method of providing value to your readers.

❏ ANSWER QUESTIONS

If you keep an eye on your audience, you'll uncover ongoing questions that they have. Use your blog posts as a way to answer the questions that resonate best with them. Questions can come from social media, blog comments and even from blog posts on other sites. Document these questions so you can refer back to them as you write new blog posts of your own.

❏ PROVIDE SOLUTIONS

There is no shortage of people looking for solutions to problems. The best and most popular blogs are often the solution-oriented variety. Give your visitors ways to do, improve or accomplish whatever it is that fits within your industry.

❏ INFORM (TEACH)

If nothing else, your blog posts should teach your visitors something new, or provide a new way of looking at a particular topic. Your visitors should always leave your blog feeling as if they learned something they didn't know before.

❏ STAY ON POINT

Keep your blog focused on your primary industry genre. While it's okay to branch out on occasion, or to throw a personal post in every now and then, for the most part, stay on point. Blogs that try to do too much, or reach too wide of an audience, have a difficult time pleasing anybody. Stay focused, and you'll please most people most of the time.

❏ INTEGRATE KEYWORDS

Each blog should be keyword focused. Perform keyword research before you start writing so you can be sure to incorporate the language that people are searching for, related to that specific blog topic, into your post. The more in-depth keyword research you perform, the more opportunities you have to rank for search queries your audience is using.

❏ WRITE NATURALLY

Your blog is an extension of your business and your authors at the same time. The last thing you want is to write in a manner that isn't reflective of both. Use natural—not keyword-stuffed—language, and be both personal and engaging. Keep your writing conversational rather than using corporate-speak.

❏ PROVIDE ACTIONABLE INSIGHTS

While some blog posts are meant to be opinion-oriented in nature, the majority of your posts should provide actionable tips and insights. Give your visitors a way to implement whatever it is they learned in each post.

❏ BE UNIQUE

If you're not blogging to provide your own unique perspective, then there is no reason to blog at all. You need to provide content, thoughts and ideas that readers cannot get anywhere else. Be unique, or pack up and go home. Look for a new angle or idea that readers will only get from you.

❏ VARY CONTENT

There are all kinds of blog posts to write, so don't get stuck in a rut of writing only one kind. Look for opportunities to provide different types of blog content to your readers. You can inform, question, shock, urge, solicit or entertain, just to name a few options. Mix it up a bit to keep your readers guessing as to what you might write next.

Example
Follow this link to see 75 different types of content you can post to your blog: http://ppmkg.com/contentplanner

❏ EXCEED EXPECTATIONS

It's not enough to give visitors what they want. You have to meet and exceed all their expectations. There are plenty of other bloggers that continually surprise their audience. People repeatedly visit blogs that are better than the rest. You need to be better than everyone else in your industry, exceeding even your own expectations for quality, engagement and education.

❏ LINK OUT

When referencing other blogs, authoritative resources, or a particular piece of content your readers might like, be sure to link out to these sources. Don't always try to keep your visitor on your site. Instead, bill yourself as the resource of resources, by providing quality information of your own, while also linking out to other sources that have information you don't.

> **Example**
> *For more checklists on web marketing, check out Pole Position Marketing's <u>Best Damn Web Marketing Cheat Sheet!</u>*

❏ CALL TO ACTION

Don't be afraid to include a call to action in each of your blog posts. This might be a call to comment, socialize, view a product or download a new information guide. Without any call to action, when the visitor has finished reading your post, they have nothing to do but leave. A good call to action will guide your visitors where you want them to go next.

❏ ADD MEDIA

Use differing forms of media to keep your blog posts interesting. This includes adding video, audio, interactive tools and more. Each type of content allows for different media options. Determine which options you can afford and will provide the most engagement for any particular blog post, and incorporate it.

❑ PROOF

When you've finished your blog post, you're not done. It's generally a good idea to let your new post sit for a couple days before you revisit and proof it. This gives you time to get away from what you thought you wrote and reread it for what you actually wrote. Then rewrite anything that is unclear, and fix any spelling and grammatical errors you find. For an even better post, have someone else proof it again before you publish it.

❑ SHARE

You should already be actively engaged on one or more social networks. Once your post is published, share it. If you've done a good job engaging with your audience, you'll likely see your post get shared a number of times, pushing it in front of an even broader audience than what you reach alone.

❑ SYNDICATE YOUR POSTS

There are a number of websites that allow you to republish your posts on their platform. While mass blog syndication can have harmful side effects, there can be a time and place for it. Sites such as LinkedIn can be used to publish an intro with a link back to the full post. Consider the pros and cons of syndication to see if it's right for you, and make sure you select your syndication platform wisely.

❑ MEASURE SUCCESS

The last step of blogging is to measure the success of each post. Measuring your successes and failures will allow you to learn what works and what posts get the most reader interest and engagement. If necessary, update your goals to make them more realistic, or, if you exceeded your own expectations, set new goals to achieve.

SOCIAL MARKETING

> Well positioned URLs have a high number of likes, shares, tweets and plus ones and specific URLs stand out in the top search results with a very high mass of social signals. On one hand this means that the activity on social networks continues to increase, on the other hand it means that frequently shared content increasingly correlates with good rankings.[34]
>
> –Searchmetrics

What This Checklist Is About

Having a "social" company means doing more than setting up a bunch of social accounts. You must also interact with your audience on each of the social platforms you've invested in, and do so in a way that generates the most value for your business. This checklist covers general social media marketing tips and ways to build up your social network profiles, in order to give your business the best social exposure possible.

Why Social Marketing Is Important

Social sharing and other "signals" from social media continue to play an increasingly significant role in obtaining top search engine rankings. Even if there is never a direct correlation between social likes, shares, and tweets, one thing we know for sure is that the more your content is shared, the more traffic and promotion it receives. That promotion—whether it comes in the form of links or exposure to a wider audience—provides signals to the search engine algorithms that tie back to ranking improvement.

In addition to any SEO value that social media can bring to your site, social media marketing provides incredible branding opportunity, customer outreach and review generation. On top of that, socialization of your content is sure to increase traffic to your website or blog, and ultimately, lead to increased sales and customer retention.

The social media landscape changes on a daily basis and there are hundreds of social networking sites your business could become active on. It's up to you to determine which sites will provide the best ROI for your business. Don't feel like you have to be fully engaged in all social channels; find those that make the most sense for your business, commit to them and be effective at building your social presence there.

SOCIAL MARKETING CHECKLIST

❏ BUILD A STRATEGY

The worst reason to participate in social media is because everyone else is doing it. Building a social strategy should be the first step you take before you even create your first social profile. Starting with your business goals and buyer personas, develop a plan with tactics that will help you reach those goals and gain new customers. This is also a good time to determine which metrics will tie into your goals and will be used to track progress and measure success.

❏ CUSTOMIZE NAMES AND URLS

When choosing your usernames, vanity names and custom URLs, it is best practice to use the same name across all channels. It is often difficult (or impossible) to change your vanity names once they are established without losing data or visitors. Think ahead and be sure you choose a name that is available across all the platforms you plan to use. Due to character limitations, keeping the same name is not always possible, but by planning ahead, you should be able to find one that is relatively consistent across all. Also, be sure to avoid the use of hyphens or special characters where possible.

Examples
Company Name: *Pole Position Marketing*
LinkedIn: *pole-position-marketing*
Facebook: *PolePositionMarketing*
Twitter: *@PolePositionMkg*
Google+: *+PolePositionMarketing*
YouTube: *PolePositionMKG*

❏ STAKE YOUR CLAIM

With literally dozens of viable social networks your business could use, it can sometimes be impossible to be active on every one of them. But it doesn't hurt to stake your claim!

The last thing you want is to find yourself in a bind if your preferred name got snapped up because you didn't take a few minutes to grab it yourself when you had the chance! Or worse, a competitor, disgruntled customer or some pesky teenager with too much time on their hands decided to create an account with your business's name—and won't let you have it.

Plan ahead and register your business name (or whatever vanity name you decide) on the "other" social networks, even if you don't plan to be active on them today.

❏ CLAIM SOCIAL REVIEW SITE LISTINGS

It's very possible that there could already be listings for your business on social review sites like Yelp or TripAdvisor. Search for your business on all of the major social review sites and make sure to claim your listing, even if you don't plan to actively use them. It's better for you have control of these rather than someone else.

❏ COMPLETE YOUR PROFILES

All social network profiles allow you to add varying business details, pictures and other company data. Make sure you complete your profile as close to 100% as possible. Always link to your website if the option is available. The more complete your profile is on any social network, the more apt that network is to benefit your business.

❏ INCLUDE KEYWORDS

When filling out your profiles or posting on your social pages, don't forget to integrate your keywords into the content. No stuffing, please!

❏ BUILD AUTHORITY RELATIONSHIPS

Most web marketing pros agree that having your content shared by authoritative people in your industry carries valuable weight that factors into your site's performance in the search results. Build relationships with people in your industry who are active on social media and have the most robust social communities. Those relationships can lead to great interaction, ideas and even new business, not to mention greater social reach.

❏ MONITOR YOUR NETWORKS

Make sure you are monitoring your social networks and social review sites for mentions of your business. Look for opportunities to actively participate in the conversations about your brand. Monitoring services such as Google Alerts, Social Mention, TalkWalker and Mention can provide a goldmine of information to score big in the reputation management department.

❏ GIVE CUSTOMERS A REASON TO FOLLOW YOU

Social networks are not a place to constantly push your latest sale or product. To succeed on social and increase social signals, you must consistently provide remarkable content that gives your customers a reason to follow you. Educate and entertain your customers. 70-80% of the content you share should be non-promotional in nature.

❏ GROW YOUR NETWORKS ORGANICALLY

Of course, you want to let your customers know you are on social media and encourage them to join you. However, running generic ads to increase likes and follows can be dangerous if not targeted with laser focus, and even then it can backfire on you. When it comes to building your following, think quality over quantity. And by all means, don't buy likes or followers. Sure, you can get 10,000 new likes or follows overnight for a mere $100, but the damage it will do to your engagement ratio is irrevocable.

❏ SOCIAL ADS

Social ads provide opportunities to reach a larger audience and increase engagement on your social channels for a fraction of the cost of running ads in search engines. This can be especially beneficial for promoting events or relevant content to specific audiences that you wouldn't be able to reach otherwise.

YOUTUBE VIDEO OPTIMIZATION

> While you may think of YouTube as more of a social networking site than a search engine, it does contain search engine functions. By utilizing the tools available for video optimization for search, you can earn more views and reach a wider audience. If you do it right, you can even get your YouTube videos to rank in Google searches.[35]
>
> –Ian Cleary
> RazorSocial

WHAT THIS CHECKLIST IS ABOUT

Optimization doesn't begin and end on your website. If you're posting videos on YouTube, they also should be optimized to help increase their presence in search engines, YouTube search and as a related video when viewers are watching related YouTube videos from other YouTube channels and your own. This checklist covers the basics of YouTube video optimization to help drive more relevant traffic to your videos.

WHY YOUTUBE VIDEO OPTIMIZATION IS IMPORTANT

YouTube videos account for the vast majority of the videos that appear in Google's Universal Search results, and YouTube is commonly declared the second largest search engine after Google. Many businesses miss the boat by uploading their videos without adding optimized titles and sometimes adding no video description at all.

In addition to the search benefits gained from optimizing your YouTube videos, optimization can also help your video appear as a suggested video after other videos or alongside them. Wouldn't it be great if your video appeared alongside a competitor's?

Just like SEO for your website, YouTube's algorithms have changed and will continue to change over time. While new factors may come into play and we don't cover every single ranking factor, this checklist will provide you with the basics that your competitors most likely haven't even thought about.

YOUTUBE VIDEO OPTIMIZATION CHECKLIST

❏ KEYWORD RESEARCH

The keywords and phrases people use to search for websites in search engines aren't always the same as the keywords and phrases they're using to search for videos. Make sure that you're using keywords that people are using on YouTube by utilizing YouTube keyword research tools such as Google Trends, Keywordtool.io or VidIQ.

❏ COMPLETE YOUR YOUTUBE CHANNEL PROFILE

Complete all available fields in your YouTube profile. Make sure you have a description, links to your website and other social profiles, channel tags that incorporate keywords for your business, cover art and profile image.

❏ ASSOCIATE YOUR WEBSITE WITH YOUR CHANNEL

In your channel settings, associate your website with your YouTube channel. This will allow you to link to URLs on your website from within your YouTube videos via cards and end cards.

❏ CLAIM YOUR VANITY URL

While YouTube has certain restrictions and qualifications your channel must meet before you can claim a vanity URL, once you have met those, be sure to claim this. It is best practice to keep your vanity URL (username) the same or similar to those used on other social networks.

Example

https://www.facebook.com/PolePositionMarketing
https://www.youtube.com/user/PolePositionMarketing

❏ ENCOURAGE CHANNEL SUBSCRIPTIONS

Increase subscriptions to your channel by utilizing the watermark feature in your channel settings. The logo becomes a watermark and clickable subscribe link on all of your videos. Take advantage of the subscribe option on end cards and add a link to your YouTube channel from your website.

❏ VIDEO FILE NAME

Before uploading your videos to YouTube, make sure your keywords are included in the file name for the video.

❏ VIDEO TITLE

Video titles should include keywords for SEO, but they should also be engaging and encourage the click. Use your main keyword or phrase at the beginning of your video title and keep your title to 70 characters or less.

❏ VIDEO DESCRIPTION

This is one of the most underutilized fields in YouTube video SEO. You've got up to 5,000 characters of space. Put them to good use! The first 160 characters of your description will serve as the meta description for your video. Keep this in mind when writing your description. Below your initial intro (meta description) you can include a transcript from your video or a detailed summary. URLs also become hyperlinks in YouTube descriptions. Include 2-3 links within your description.

❏ VIDEO TAGS

Include related keywords and keyword variations in your video tags. Also include the names of your competitors in your tags and other channels that are ranking well for the keyword.

❑ VIDEO CAPTIONS

YouTube creates automatic captions for videos, but they are often grossly inaccurate. Just Google "YouTube caption fails." Search engines can't "read" the content of your video, but they can "read" the content of your captions. Utilize a caption service such as Speechpad to easily and economically create professional captions for your videos.

❑ VIDEO THUMBNAIL

While a custom video thumbnail doesn't have a direct impact on video rankings, it can help encourage the click to watch your video over a competitor's.

❑ VIDEO QUALITY

Videos recorded in HD tend to rank better than SD videos. In addition to the technical quality of your video recording, make sure your video sound quality is good. The easier your video is to watch and hear, the more likely people are to watch it—and watch time is a prominent factor in video rankings.

❑ VIDEO ENGAGEMENT

Make sure your videos engage the user and keep their attention. YouTube looks at how long people have watched your video and other engagement metrics such as comments, likes and shares.

❑ VIDEO CARDS & END CARDS

Utilize features such as cards and end cards to engage the user and keep them interested in your channel and other YouTube videos.

ONLINE PR / LINK MARKETING

> Building relationships is the ever-present advice from our experts. If you want to build links, you've got to build relationships with the people behind the sites. People, not websites, make links.[36]
>
> –BuzzStream

WHAT THIS CHECKLIST IS ABOUT

No longer is counting the number of links an effective measure of link building efforts. Search engines are actively changing their algorithms to account for more natural link building methods while discounting any method that is deemed to be manipulative. Rather than focusing on links for the sake of links, this checklist covers important aspects of online relationship building and link marketing that help you earn links organically. You'll learn how to build relationships that can turn into valuable earned links and social shares, both of which are important in today's search algorithms.

WHY ONLINE PR AND LINK MARKETING ARE IMPORTANT

Search engines are forever looking at signals that tell them how important or authoritative a particular website (or web page) is for any given search query. In the past, how many websites linked to you (and the quality of those sites) weighed heavily in the search algorithms. The problem with using links as an algorithmic measure was that the bar to achieve a link was pretty high. A business just had to have a website of its own in order to create a link back to your site.

The invention of blogs lowered that bar a bit. While it may seem like everyone and their dog has a blog, it's just not the case. And many people (not necessarily businesses) are no longer going through the hassle to set up a blog in favor of posting on social media instead.

Today, millions more people are active on social media than those that actively publish blog posts. Built into these social accounts is the ability to like, share or talk about things that are important to the individual. In fact, that's why social sites were built. Search engines understand this and want to factor these conversations into their algorithms. Social signals provide the search engines with more—and better—signals to gauge the value of the business being discussed.

Online PR is the process of utilizing social media for building relationships, and then leveraging those relationships to build trust for your site in the form of links and shares. As with most relationships, if you set out only to manipulate, you will likely fail and/or your efforts will backfire. Any attempt to "use" the partners in the relationship won't work for long. Your online relationships must be mutually beneficial in order to be maintained. If you build them correctly, those relationships can turn into links, shares, likes and other social signals the search engine algorithms value.

ONLINE PR/ LINK MARKETING CHECKLIST

❏ FIND INFLUENCERS

Research similar, related and corresponding niche industries to find the right influencers. These influencers are actively using social media, having generated a good number of followers. You should notice that their content is regularly shared and re-shared by their connections. Use tools such as Klout and Kred to assess the value of each influencer and to determine whether making a connection with them will add value to your social and link marketing goals.

❏ LISTEN

Shhhh. Stop talking! At least for right now. Take some time and just listen to (i.e., read) the conversations your influencers are having between themselves and their followers. Seek to understand the best ways—and best ways not—to interact. This is also a good time to read what content influencers are sharing, as it will help you understand what content resonates best with other influencers and the audience you want to be influencing.

❏ SET-UP KEYWORD ALERTS

Set up alerts for a few of your top-priority keywords. Tools like Google Alerts and Moz Fresh Alerts can help you stay abreast of what others in your industry are sharing and posting with the keywords that are important to you. Seeing what content others are posting will help you find new influencers and give you an arena in which to become an influencer yourself.

❏ SELECT INFLUENCERS TO ENGAGE

It's a good idea to choose only a handful of influencers to focus your engagement efforts on. Building relationships takes time, and you want to be able to fully engage with a few top influencers rather than half-heartedly engage with many. Stay current on their social shares, blog posts and other information they find valuable. Gain as much knowledge about these influencers as possible.

❏ SHARE INFLUENCER CONTENT

If you want others to share your content, you need to share their content first. Find content topically related to your sphere, written by your industry's influencers, and share it with your connections. While social media can be valuable for sharing your own content, you want to avoid being known as a self-promoter. In general, you should regularly share 70% of other people's content verses 30% of your own.

❏ ENGAGE

Start engaging the influencers by replying to their social comments and adding comments of your own to their blog posts and streams. Seek to build quality relationships, making sure your interactions are thoughtful and add value to the conversation. Don't act like a fanboy or try to promote yourself in any way. As you build genuine relationships, those you are engaging will figure out who you are and what you do.

Examples
No: *What a great post! I read almost everything you write and, as usual, you're dead on!*

No: *Awesome idea! I wrote about something similar here.*

Yes: *Great post! I have a similar approach but I think yours connects a few dots that I might have been missing. What do you think about...?*

❏ MAXIMIZE YOUR NETWORK

Once you have established legitimate relationships through social sharing and commentary, you can begin to seek a little something for yourself. On occasion, you can approach an influencer to ask them to share some specific content that they might find valuable for themselves or their audience.

Depending on your relationship, you can ask for something as simple as a share or retweet. If you have a more solid relationship, you might ask them to share your content, adding their own thoughts, or maybe even link to your content from their blog. Don't abuse your relationships by seeking your own promotion too often. And always be willing to continue to share other's content regardless of whether or not they promote everything you ask.

❏ EXPAND YOUR NETWORK

Continue nurturing your existing social relationships while finding additional influencers you can establish new relationships with. Don't spread yourself too thin. Grow your network slowly as you have the time to read, learn and engage. Only ask for help with promoting your own content after each relationship is sufficiently established.

PAY-PER-CLICK ADVERTISING

> Google follows your campaign settings to determine where, when and how you would like those ads displayed. If you would like keywords or ads displayed differently based on varying conditions, then you need a different campaign for each of those conditions.[37]
>
> –Brad Geddes
> *Advanced Google AdWords*

What This Checklist Is About

This checklist covers pay-per-click (PPC) account set up and campaign management procedures. Setting up a PPC campaign can be relatively easy to do, but achieving the proper ROI can be difficult. As a result, there are strategies to setting up and managing a PPC campaign that are not inherently obvious. These strategies can be critical to running a profitable advertising and marketing campaign.

Why Pay-Per-Click Advertising Is Important

Many PPC account managers improperly analyze campaign performance, creating false conclusions about the value of their PPC marketing efforts. Ultimately, they fail at maximizing their return on investment, leading them to believe that PPC isn't profitable. Rarely is there a PPC campaign that can't be made profitable, but it takes proper set-up and management to make it work.

Many PPC campaigns fail, not from the lack of profitable possibilities, but by the manager's lack of understanding in how to leverage those possibilities effectively.

Proper PPC account set-up and campaign management can be the difference between a successful campaign and one that costs more than it earns. As you engage in PPC, it is important to follow key practices, understanding the value of each click and sale in relation to the amount of traffic being delivered at what price.

When you have a handle on the cost of each click, in relation to the profit achieved, you are better able to manage your ad groups and campaigns effectively. This helps you ensure each click to your site is a profitable one.

PAY-PER-CLICK ADVERTISING CHECKLIST

❏ CALCULATE CONVERSION VALUE

List all of the actions visitors can accomplish on your site that will either add revenue or reduce cost to the business. Assign a value to each these macro- and micro-conversions so you are able to calculate the net profit of each.

❏ LINK ACCOUNTS

Link your Google AdWords and Analytics accounts together. This allows your Google Analytics account to automatically import AdWords data into the correct reports, giving you a fuller range of reporting data with fewer steps.

❏ ENABLE AUTO-TAGGING

AdWords auto-tagging allows you to automatically tag each of your destination URLs with campaign parameters that will be imported into Google Analytics. Tagging your URLs ensures that the pre-click AdWords data can be combined with the post-click data in your Analytics.

❏ INSTALL CONVERSION TRACKING

Use your web analytics tool and your PPC platform's conversion tracking capabilities to tie conversions and values to your campaigns. Without these tie-ins, you have no real metric for determining a true value for each conversion.

❏ SEPARATE CAMPAIGNS

Search and Display Network campaigns are very different and demand different strategies, budgets, etc. Create specific campaigns for each to allow for maximized bidding and ROI improvement strategies.

❏ PROPER AD CAMPAIGN/AD GROUP USAGE

Set up *campaigns* using general keyword themes and *ad groups* using more specific keywords. For example, your *campaign* could be "Motorcycle Batteries" and your *ad groups* might be "BMW Motorcycle Batteries," "Harley Motorcycle Batteries," etc.

❏ PROPERLY ORGANIZE CAMPAIGNS

Spend time carefully organizing your campaigns. The goal is to perfectly align questions with answers. Every query should produce an ad that directly addresses the query's topic, issues, intents and desires, as well as directs the searcher to the most appropriate page.

❏ ADS MATCH INTENT

Write ads that match the searcher's intent and include a clear benefit to the seeker. Don't use marketing lingo in your search ads. The more you can match what the searcher is looking for with words that pique their interest, the better your ads will perform.

❏ UTILIZE AD EXTENSIONS

Use ad extensions to improve the performance of your ads. Ad extensions allow you to provide additional information and functionality within each ad. For example, *sitelink* extensions add more links to your site under the ad, and *call extensions* add a phone number that searchers can use to call your business. Utilize the extensions that will most benefit the searcher and your business.

❏ USE KEYWORD MATCH TYPES PROPERLY

Keyword match types control how ads are matched to the search queries being performed. Every ad can be matched to *broad, phrase* or *exact* keywords. Failure to implement these match types correctly can be very costly. Also, be sure to pay attention to *negative* keywords in order to keep your ads from showing on irrelevant searches.

❏ ANALYZE BIDDING STRATEGIES

Analyze and adjust your bids based upon location, time and device. Make sure you are bidding at a granular level to maximize your ROI. For example, if the US performs 20% better than average and Canada 20% worse than average, you might adjust the bidding in those locations by +20% and -20% respectively.

❏ TEST ADS AND LANDING PAGES

Always be testing your ads and landing pages by creating multiple variations of each. Test them against each other to find what your customers respond to the best. Over time, you'll achieve better campaign performance, reducing costs and increasing revenue at the same time.

❏ TAKE ADVANTAGE OF REMARKETING

Be sure to use *remarketing* options to target PPC ads to web users who have previously visited your site, but are currently elsewhere on the web. By default, remarketed (or retargeted) campaigns garner the best ROI among PPC opportunities because of their highly targeted nature. Set up campaigns for both the search and display networks to capitalize on those conversions.

❏ CREATE BID STRATEGY OPTIONS

Create multiple bid strategy options to apply to your campaigns, ad groups and keywords. Over time, you'll want to adjust bids by performance. Flexible bidding strategies (in AdWords) allow you to do this at all levels of your campaign. Make sure your bid strategy options are guided by your advertising goals.

❏ CREATE BRAND KEYWORD CAMPAIGNS

There are many reasons to secure the very top spot in the paid search results for branded keywords. A brand campaign gives you the ability to control your message, protect your real estate and prevent competitors from stealing clicks. Brand keyword click costs are often ultra-cheap because your quality score on these campaigns will be very high.

❏ STUDY YOUR COMPETITORS

Study your competitors and make adjustments to your campaigns as needed. If you don't know your opponents, it's difficult to beat them. Studying their ads, landing pages, ad positions, impression share, etc., can give insight that helps you make smarter decisions on your campaigns.

EMAIL MARKETING

Email remains a powerful way to connect with customers and influence their buying decisions: 66% of online Americans say they have made a purchase as a result of an email from a brand, more than three times the percentage of people who have purchased in response to a message delivered via Facebook (20%) or text message (16%).[38]

–MarketingProfs

WHAT THIS CHECKLIST IS ABOUT

True email marketing is more than writing a message and broadcasting it to a list of hundreds or thousands of subscribers. Email marketing should not be used solely as a broadcast medium, but as a point of engagement with your audience. The points in this checklist will help you get the most from your email marketing campaign, avoiding typical pitfalls that don't work or might even get you flagged as a spammer, and will help you increase your email open, click-thru and engagement rates.

WHY EMAIL MARKETING IS IMPORTANT

Email marketing can be one of the most effective forms of online marketing. You first must have a strong list of people interested in receiving your emails, and then you must execute your content creation and delivery properly. The idea behind email marketing is to take your list of individuals who have "subscribed" to your company updates, deliver what they expect and then work to keep them engaged with your brand.

The dangers of email marketing can be significant. Many who opt-in may later forget they had done so, and subsequently mark your message as spam. Or, those who have opted in no longer feel you are delivering what you promised, and again, mark your message as spam. To prevent your emails from being flagged, you must have a great message, and it must be exactly what the receiver wants and expects from you. Any deviation (with few exceptions) can get you into trouble.

Email marketing doesn't have to be expensive, but it does need to be executed properly. There is no sense sending out mass emails if no one wants or cares about what you're sending. This is your chance to engage with your audience, so make sure your message is engaging, not just a sales pitch for your brand.

When you craft smart messages and use email marketing wisely, you open up new opportunities for your customers to interact with your company. However, since email marketing is more "in-your-face" than other forms of online marketing, great care must be taken to do it right.

EMAIL MARKETING CHECKLIST

❏ CREATE AN INTEGRATED PLAN

As with all other forms of marketing, you need to first create an email marketing strategy that can be seamlessly integrated with your other online and offline marketing activities. All marketing activities should support each other, and email marketing is no exception to this rule. Nothing screws up the scent more than an email message that is not carried through onto the landing page.

❏ SELECT AN EMAIL MARKETING SERVICE

Sending mass emails through your own email client can cause all sorts of problems. Chances are your emails won't look as professional as they should, and will be much more likely to be flagged as spam. Using an email marketing service such as MailChimp, AWeber or Constant Contact will give you better deliverability rates, a more professional look, list management tools and additional analytics, just to name a few benefits.

❏ NATURAL TEXT, NOT IMAGE TEXT

Many email clients do not automatically download images with the message. Make sure that you provide the bulk of your content in natural text so that email subscribers can read the message even if the images are not loaded. If too much text is used in images, your message is also more likely to get caught in spam filters. Images should support your text, not be your text.

❏ TEXT VERSION

Provide a text-only version of your email. Many email readers will mangle your template, rendering it difficult to read. Provide a link to a text version and/or provide the option of subscribing to the text version instead of the HTML version of the email.

❏ DON'T SPAM

Never add someone to your email list without their permission. Having your email messages marked as spam by a large number of recipients will make it more difficult for you to get your message to the people that really count—not to mention opening yourself up to fines under the CAN-SPAM Act. It's a good idea to qualify subscribers by having them double opt-in to your email list. This will help you cut down on spam reports and bounces.

❏ AVOID SPAM TRIGGERS

Avoid common email spam triggers such as using all caps, excessive punctuation, sloppy HTML, no text (text only in images) and overusing certain words that are typically used by spammers. Review your message for all of these triggers and any others that become commonplace over time. Staying on top of new spam triggers is important to ensure your messages continue to reach your audience.

Examples

No: DOWNLOAD A FREE COPY TODAY!

No: *That's right!!! You can download your free copy today!!!!*

No: *An affordable bargain that puts more $$$ in your pocket with a money-back guarantee!*

❑ BE CONSISTENT

While your subscribers may not want to hear from you every two hours, it's also important to be consistent in your message delivery. If you only email your list once every six months, they may forget they signed up to receive your emails in the first place, marking your emails as spam. Survey your subscribers and customers to find out how often they want to hear from you. You may be surprised: It might be more often, or not as often, as you think!

It's also important to keep your email design consistent. As with all other aspects of marketing, you want your emails to be an easily recognizable extension of your brand. Don't change the overall design of your email unless absolutely necessary.

❑ PROPER REPLY-TO ADDRESS AND "FROM" NAME

Don't use a reply-to address from a generic email account. Rather, use your company's domain-based email address. Larger businesses may want to send messages from a unique email address specific for these broadcasts, with the message using your company as the "from name." If you're a smaller business, make it more personal. Send your message using the real name and email address of someone well known. Whichever way you go, choose one email address to use and stick with it.

Email Address Examples
No: *sgd@gmail.com*
Yes: *newsletter@polepositionmarketing.com*
Yes: *stoney@polepositionmarketing.com*

"From Name" Examples
No: *Auto-Message*
Yes: *Pole Position Marketing*
Yes: *Stoney deGeyter*

❑ CREATE AN AMAZING SUBJECT LINE

A great subject line will increase your email open rates and discourage uninterested readers from flagging messages as spam. Just like titles of blog posts, your email subject line should immediately grab your subscribers' attention. This is your big chance to get your message read.

The subject line must tell subscribers what they will find when they open your email. Also, incorporate a call to action when possible. Keep your most important information at the beginning, and try and keep the entire subject line to fewer than 50 characters.

Examples
No: *How to Create an Effective Email Campaign.*
Yes: *Email Campaigns that Make Business Boom!*

❏ EXCELLENT CONTENT

The content of your email should be relevant, useful and timely. Stay focused on your message and don't try to achieve too many objectives at once. You are building a long-term relationship, so don't abuse the permission your audience has given you to send them messages. Your email content should be skimmable and easy to read. Use web-safe fonts (such as Arial or Verdana), and highlight text using bold or bulleted copy instead of italics, which can be more difficult to read.

❏ PROOF, PROOF, PROOF

Unlike a web page that can be edited after you've published it, once you hit "send" on an email message, there's no taking it back. Make sure you thoroughly proofread before sending. It's not a bad idea to have one or two other people proof and edit each message as well. If that's not possible, read it aloud to yourself to make sure it says what you intend.

❏ RUN TESTS

After you've proofed your email, send yourself a test message. Make sure that the graphics and text look correct, and re-read your message once again. Often, you'll find errors that you missed before. View your email message in different browsers and on mobile devices to ensure it's readable across the board. If you have a large enough subscriber list, send out small-scale tests with differing subject lines, headlines, calls to action, etc., to gauge open and click-through rates. Pick the winning message and send that to the rest of your list.

❏ TRACK YOUR SUCCESS

Growing your subscriber list is important, but there are other metrics that should be tracked as well. Most email marketing services provide a way to add Google Analytics tracking codes to each link in your message. This helps you track how your subscribers interact with every email they receive and your website.

Track both open and site click-through rates. As you track, document which things work better than others so you can use that information to improve on each subsequent message, increasing reader interaction over time. Your goal is to decrease bounce and unsubscribe rates, while increasing the number of receivers who click through to your site and convert.

ANALYTICS ISSUES

Our first tactic when we want more of something…is
to stress how important a project is. It never works.
[Great analytics] changes the conversation from "go
away" to "How can I help you be more successful?"[39]
—Avinash Kaushik
Web Analytics 2.0

WHAT THIS CHECKLIST IS ABOUT

This checklist covers how to set up a Google Analytics account, along with analytic tracking best practices. Google Analytics is a free and easy-to-use platform that many businesses have adopted for tracking their website's performance. While this checklist focuses primarily on Google Analytics implementation, many of these tips can be used with any analytics platform.

WHY ANALYTICS IS IMPORTANT

If you're going to make informed decisions about how to improve your website's performance, visitor data is essential. It's not enough to "feel" like things are improving. You must truly know what is (or isn't) working and why. As exciting as it is to see a surge of new sales as a result of your online marketing efforts, that data alone isn't enough to help you make informed decisions. There is more to your website's data than you might intuitively know, and unless you're looking at it with the proper eye, you're likely missing out on some good stuff.

Analytics is less about studying numbers and graphs than it is about letting your website traffic tell you a story. That story can give you some great insight into how to turn a small increase in business into a much larger increase in business. Yes, you can always strive to get more traffic, but what if you could get a greater number of your *existing* visitors to buy your products or services?

That's the goal of looking at your analytics and engaging in conversion optimization. Take the visitors you have and learn how to get more of them to become customers. It's about finding out where and why people leave your site and patching up the holes that cause them to escape. It's about finding new and better ways to keep them engaged and moving them through the conversion process.

Without analytics and conversion optimization processes in place, you're losing money every day by not converting the visitors who would otherwise become your customers. Instead, you have to rely on increasing your budget to drive more traffic to your site, rather than making your site better for the traffic you already have. While there is nothing wrong with getting more traffic, converting more traffic reaps greater rewards.

ANALYTICS ISSUES CHECKLIST

❏ SET UP ANALYTICS ACCOUNT

There are many analytic platforms you can choose from, but Google provides a very robust, free and easy-to-implement tool that is a great place to begin. Whatever platform you choose, be sure to implement the correct code into your website and ensure all permissions are set so appropriate team members in your organization have necessary access.

❏ TRACK GOALS

You want to measure the visitor actions that bring you success. What are the reasons your site exists? What do you want your visitors to do? These are your goals you want to keep an eye on so if they improve or fail, you know about it. Set up each of these goals in your analytics and make sure the data is being recorded whenever a visitor reaches or achieves these goals.

❑ **CALCULATE ECONOMIC VALUE**

Assess your goals and identify the increase in revenue or reduction in cost each creates for the business. Enter this data as your goal values so you can determine the overall impact each goal has on your business.

❑ **TRACK INTERNAL SITE SEARCH**

When people search using your site's internal search box, they are astonishingly precise about what they want. Capture this data for analysis and use it to determine what is important to your visitors. From there you can begin to improve your site's overall performance accordingly.

❑ **SET UP CUSTOM ALERTS**

When something interesting is happening on your site, you want to know about it right away. This is especially true if a critical action must be taken. Set up analytics alerts so you have the opportunity to react to "irregular" events quickly, either to capitalize on a success or to avoid a potential disaster.

❑ **EXCLUDE INTERNAL TRAFFIC**

When analyzing your traffic data, you don't want to include visits from your internal team. After all, they are not your target audience and are likely interacting with your site for entirely different reasons. Be sure to exclude traffic that comes from inside of your organization so your analysis isn't skewed by this data.

❑ **EXCLUDE UNWANTED / SPAM TRAFFIC**

Along with internal team traffic, you also want to look at other unwanted or spammy traffic sources. Make sure you set up filters for these as well so you don't end up with false data. When analyzing your traffic, you want to focus on regular site visitors and users.

❑ **LINK ANALYTICS TO SEARCH CONSOLE**

If you use Google Analytics, link it with your Google Search Console account. This allows Search Console data to be imported directly into the Analytics search engine optimization reports for deeper analysis.

❏ INSTALL ECOMMERCE TRACKING

Where applicable, install ecommerce tracking codes so you can track metrics such as transactions, revenue and average sale value. This data can be extremely important as you determine the value of each visitor. It also provides insight on how best to funnel your advertising and marketing budgets to reach those that bring the highest profits.

❏ KEEP ANNOTATIONS

Make notes (annotations) on your analytics timeline when significant events occur that might affect your site's performance. For example, overhauling your navigation, optimizing a page, achieving a significant increase in search rankings, or even performing off-site marketing should all be noted with start/stop dates where applicable. This allows you to reference back to see how particular events impacted your traffic and conversions.

❏ CREATE CUSTOM REPORTS & DASHBOARDS

Use your analytics tool to build dashboards that will allow you to create custom, automated reports. These reports should focus on your most important metrics and segments of traffic. This will help you focus on what's most valuable to your business, making analysis and action quicker and easier as you move forward.

CONCLUDING REMARKS

After producing such an exhaustive list of things to do, I'm not sure there is anything left to say. Once you've downloaded the companion Cheat Sheet (WebMarketingChecklist.com), you have everything you need: Your check-list, your action points, and a whole lot of work ahead of you. No sense belaboring that any longer. Go on. Get to work making your site the best damn website your niche has ever seen. Period!

PS. If all this makes you feel a little overwhelmed I suggest you take it one check- list at a time. If that's still too much, contact the Pit Crew at Pole Position Marketing (info@pole-positionmarketing.com) and get help from the experts.

RESOURCES

1. URL as UI: http://www.nngroup.com/articles/url-as-ui/

2. I don't care about Responsive Web Design: http://stuffandnonsense.co.uk/blog/about/i_dont_care_about_responsive_web_design/

3. Mobile Usability: http://www.amazon.com/dp/0321884485

4. Don't Make Me Think, Revisited: A Common Sense Approach to Web Usability: https://www.amazon.com/Dont-Make-Think-Revisited-Usability/dp/0321965515/

5. Chapter 4: Site Architecture & Search Engine Success Factors: http://searchengineland.com/guide/seo/site-architecture-search-engine-ranking

6. Don't Make Me Think, Revisited: A Common Sense Approach to Web Usability: https://www.amazon.com/Dont-Make-Think-Revisited-Usability/dp/0321965515/

7. Are You Making These Common Website Navigation Mistakes?: http://blog.kissmetrics.com/common-website-navigation-mistakes/

8. Search Analytics for Your Site: https://www.amazon.com/Search-Analytics-Your-Louis-Rosenfeld-ebook/dp/B005EI86HC/

9. Everybody Writes: Your Go-To Guide to Creating Ridiculously Good Content: https://www.amazon.com/Everybody-Writes-Go-Creating-Ridiculously/dp/1118905555/

10. Web Page Design: A Different Multimedia: http://www.amazon.com/Web-Page-Design-Different-Multimedia/dp/013239880X/

11. Web Page Design: A Different Multimedia: http://www.amazon.com/Web-Page-Design-Different-Multimedia/dp/013239880X/

12. Search Engine Ranking Factors 2015: https://moz.com/search-ranking-factors/

13. The Importance of Your Homepage; Twenty-Five Seconds and Counting: http://blog.3dcart.com/the-importance-of-your-homepage-twenty-five-seconds-and-counting/

14. Why an "About Us" page is so important: https://www.rocketspark.com/blog/why-about-us-page-so-important/

15. How To Optimize Contact Forms For Conversions: http://unbounce.com/conversion-rate-optimization/how-to-optimize-contact-forms/

16. 10 Tips for Improving E-commerce Product Pages: https://econsultancy.com/us/blog/11205-10-tips-for-improving-e-commerce-product-pages

17. The Ultimate Guide to Ecommerce Category Pages: https://www.optimonk.com/ecommerce-category-pages

18. How to Build a Perfect B2B Product Page: https://blog.hubspot.com/marketing/how-to-build-perfect-b2b-product-page-ht

19. Digital Window Shopping: The Long Journey to "Buy": http://docplayer.net/16184490-Digital-window-shopping-the-long-journey-to-buy.html

20. Checkout Page Optimization: Just Follow the F.A.C.T.S.: https://moz.com/blog/checkout-page-optimization-just-follow-the-facts

21. Why Online Retailers Are Losing 67.45% of Sales and What to Do About It: https://www.shopify.com/blog/8484093-why-online-retailers-are-losing-67-45-of-sales-and-what-to-do-about-it

22. 12 Ways to Create a User-Friendly Website Registration Process: https://blog.hubspot.com/blog/tabid/6307/bid/31517/12-Ways-to-Create-a-User-Friendly-Website-Registration-Process.aspx

23. How to Make Your Form Error Messages More Reassuring: http://uxmovement.com/forms/how-to-make-your-form-error-messages-more-reassuring/

24. Get More Out of Your Thank You Pages: 4 Easy Tips: https://www.kunocreative.com/blog/bid/83349/Get-More-Out-of-Your-Thank-You-Pages-4-Easy-Tips

25. Get Your FAQs Straight: Convert Your Curious Customers: https://blog.kissmetrics.com/get-your-faqs-straight/

26. How to Craft a Privacy Policy for Your Website: http://www.socialmediaexaminer.com/how-to-craft-a-privacy-policy-for-your-website/

27. About Sitemaps: https://support.google.com/webmasters/answer/156184. Yes, I quoted Google Search Console. Get over it.

28. A Visual Guide to Keyword Targeting and On-Page Optimization: https://moz.com/blog/visual-guide-to-keyword-targeting-onpage-optimization

29. 6 Ways to Accelerate Your Local SEO Success in 2014: https://searchenginewatch.com/article/2319419/6-Ways-to-Accelerate-Your-Local-SEO-Success-in-2014

30. Landing Page Optimization: The Definitive Guide to Testing and Tuning for Conversions: https://www.amazon.com/Landing-Page-Optimization-Definitive-Conversions/dp/0470610123/

31. 10 Must Know Image Optimization Tips: https://www.shopify.com/blog/7412852-10-must-know-image-optimization-tips#axzz2o2w8Aver

32. PDF: Unfit for Human Consumption: https://www.nngroup.com/articles/pdf-unfit-for-human-consumption/

33. 13 reasons your business needs a blog: http://lifecycle-performance-pros.com/phocadownload/Resources/Blogging/Blogging-for-Business.pdf

34. SEO Ranking Factors – Rank Correlation 2013 for Google USA: http://www.searchmetrics.com/en/services/ranking-factors-2013/

35. YouTube SEO – How to Drive More Organic Traffic to Your Videos: http://www.razorsocial.com/youtube-seo/

36. Linking outside the box: Link Building Experts Share Their Secrets: http://gerommetalampas.com/Linking-Outside-the-Box.pdf

37. Advanced Google AdWords: https://www.amazon.com/Advanced-Google-AdWords-Brad-Geddes-ebook/dp/B007RSUSKA/

38. Email Content Still Most Likely to Influence Buying Decisions: http://www.marketingprofs.com/charts/2012/7584/email-content-still-most-likely-to-influence-buying-decisions

39. Web Analytics 2.0: The Art of Online Accountability and Science of Customer Centricity: https://www.amazon.com/Web-Analytics-2-0-Accountability-Centricity-ebook/dp/B0032ZD0IE/

Made in the USA
San Bernardino, CA
22 November 2019